What people are saying about ...

being real > being perfect

"Life is hard. It is for all of us ... But it doesn't have to be complicated. Finding your true self is now easier than ever with the help of my friend Justin Davis's new book. Helping you embrace the reality of who you are instead of who you pretend to be is Justin's sweet spot, and I can't wait for you to experience these words."

Carlos Whittaker, author of *How to Human*

"Ten out of ten times I will support a book about being real over being perfect, if the author is someone I know to live this message themselves. Justin Davis has done the work to earn the right to lead us in this important message of freedom and fulfillment found only in the truth of Christ. It's books like these that bring needed transparency and, as a result, healing to the Church."

Lisa Whittle, author of *Jesus Over Everything* and *God Knows*, Bible teacher, podcast host

"My friend Justin provides practical steps for readers to push back against perfectionism, embrace authenticity, and discover real transformation. This book is a must-read for anyone who struggles with self-doubt, shame, or a fear of vulnerability."

Jon Acuff, *New York Times* bestselling author of *Soundtracks: The Surprising Solution to Overthinking*

"Justin has given us one of those books that will read you better than you will read it. It is as thoughtful as it is practical as it is hopeful. Through his vulnerability, humor, and spiritual depth, this book gave me a greater desire to be more like Jesus and a clearer path to help me get there. I believe it can do the same for you."

Jarrett Stevens, copastor at
Soul City Church and author of
Praying Through and *Four Small Words*

"The journey to becoming my real, genuine self over the polished, Instagram version of me is one I've been on for the past few years. It's not easy letting other people into the messy parts of your life, but I've found firsthand that when we do, we're able to find true community and, even more so, a deeper relationship with Jesus. Justin's words give us the practical tools we need to ditch the fake versions of us—opening up to ourselves, our community, and God. This is a book I needed, and I bet it's one you need too."

Adam Weber, lead pastor of Embrace
Church, host of *The Conversation* podcast,
author of *Love Has a Name*

"Justin Davis is the real deal. It's one of the many reasons people are drawn to him and his leadership. He knows life is too short and precious to squander our time in image management. But let's be real. Being real takes courage, a plan, a path. That's what this book is about. If you're tired of wondering what people are thinking about you and being confined by what they may or may not be saying, be encouraged. There is a path to break away from this. Being *real*, being who you really are, is possible. Being perfect isn't."

Jeff Henderson, author of *What to Do Next: Taking Your Best Step When Life Is Uncertain*

"Vulnerability generates intimacy in any relationship, and this book captures that important spiritual and social ingredient better than any I've read."

Jon Weece, lead follower at Southland Christian Church

"In a culture that platforms the facade of perfection benefiting no one, my friend Justin is living a life of authenticity, loud and proud. His willingness to speak the truth about the beauty in brokenness provides all those who read this a solid resource to better live out the tension between this world and eternity. This book will help you see clearly the way God sees you—as His child created in His image."

Jenni Wong Clayville, pastor and speaker, National Community Church

"One of the things I've always appreciated about Justin in my friendship with him over the years is his willingness to be fully transparent and vulnerable in our conversations. He invites people to speak into his life so he can grow. His example inspires me to do the same. What I've grown to know of him in person I see when I read the pages of his book. Let these words encourage you, challenge you, and inspire you."

Aaron Brockett, lead pastor of Traders Point Christian Church

"Justin took a risk; he revealed his weaknesses and lived to tell about it. So many of us are afraid we might die, or worse, be abandoned, if people really knew our mistakes and missteps. I met Justin in a season when my life was falling apart. No, really it was. The way he and his wife, Trish, allowed others to see their brokenness at a marriage seminar I attended was a true example of sacrificial bravery. I took a few brave steps that night myself. Those of us in the spotlight of Christian culture MUST have permission to fail, and confess, and repent. *Being Real > Being Perfect* is a firsthand account of life after perfectionism and the community that rises up around brokenness."

Brandon Heath, Contemporary
Christian recording artist

"From an early age, we learned how to armor up, put on masks, and play a version of ourselves we thought was the acceptable one—the one most likely to succeed and not get hurt along the way. The problem is that kind of living suffocates our truest selves and leads to a life that feels trapped, unknown, and unacceptable. I'm grateful that Justin has voiced what most all of us have wrestled with at one time or another: we are made with purpose, on purpose, for a purpose, and God invites us to let down our defenses and masks to be seen and accepted as we really are."

Dave Dummitt, senior pastor of Willow
Creek Community Church

"In this Instagram, TikTok, take-a-hundred-pics-to-get-the-perfect-angle culture we live in, I believe each of our souls is crying out for something real. Justin's call to transparency invites all of us to put down the facade, let others into the mess, and finally experience true wholeness."

Davey Blackburn, author, speaker, podcaster, founder of Nothing is Wasted Ministries

"There is a life that is possible. One that is honest and human, one that experiences deep healing and transformation. But if you're like me, you can deeply struggle with knowing how to access this kind life. This is why trusted guides like Justin Davis are so helpful to show you the way and through Scripture to unpack how being relentlessly transparent can help you become everything you were always intended to be."

Steve Carter, author of *The Thing Beneath the Thing*

"There is pressure coming from all directions for us to present the best versions of ourselves. That's why I'm so grateful for this book! *Being Real > Being Perfect* is an insightful and inspiring book that encourages readers to embrace their authentic selves and let go of the burden of people pleasing. Justin Davis's personal journey and honest storytelling make this a must-read for anyone seeking the freedom that only comes from being real!"

Josh Surratt, lead pastor of Seacoast Church

"I'll never forget the day we had Justin and his wife, Trish, on our morning show. Justin was sharing a really tender part of his story when he said this: 'The worst lie is the lie you tell yourself.' That statement has stuck with me for over ten years now! Justin went on to explain that if you can't be honest with yourself, you can't be honest with anyone. If you've been in community with Justin and Trish, you know Justin doesn't just preach this message; he lives it. For all these reasons, I highly recommend *Being Real > Being Perfect* to anyone who wants to experience the grace and power of God's transforming love."

Carmen Brown, cohost of *The Morning Cruise,* The JOY FM

"Justin has a personal story that demonstrates the power of how God uses our mistakes in a way that qualifies us to later be able to better serve others. God can only use us that way if we are able to be vulnerable and share who we are with others. Read this book, as it will help give you the courage to connect with people in a deeper way and make a bigger impact in the world."

Rory Vaden, *New York Times* bestselling author of *Take the Stairs*

"We are all looking for approval, control, and security in one way or another. When we finally discover that authentic belonging doesn't depend on us adjusting who we are—it just invites us to be who we are— that's when we experience the gift of radical acceptance. Justin offers each of us an honest and hopeful road map in learning to remember that being real > being perfect."

Jeanne Stevens, founding lead pastor of Soul City Church

"Justin challenges us all to risk being authentic at the expense of not being accepted by some but living a real life with everyone. If you aspire to thrive in life and truly live at peace with God and yourself, YOU NEED TO READ THIS BOOK! The real you is waiting to meet you! This book will help catapult you into a journey of discovering your authentic self!"

Andrew "MO" Momon Jr., author of *LeaderFit* and *Be the Answer* and lead pastor of Victory Church-Midtown

"Impostor syndrome has taken over much of the world. Sadly, many churches struggle with it even more than the outside world does. Justin goes toe to toe with the shame epidemic flooding over Christians. Beyond naming the problem, this read gives tangible guidance to uncover our deepest fears and unleash greater freedom."

Dr. Tim Harlow, lead pastor at Parkview Christian Church

being
real
>
being
perfect

justin davis

being real

real

being

perfect

how transparency
leads to transformation

DAVID C COOK

transforming lives together

BEING REAL > BEING PERFECT
Published by David C Cook
4050 Lee Vance Drive
Colorado Springs, CO 80918 U.S.A.

Integrity Music Limited, a Division of David C Cook
Brighton, East Sussex BN1 2RE, England

The graphic circle C logo is a registered trademark of David C Cook.

The website addresses recommended throughout this book are offered as a
resource to you. These websites are not intended in any way to be or imply an
endorsement on the part of David C Cook, nor do we vouch for their content.

Details in some stories have been changed to protect
the identities of the persons involved.

Bible credits are listed in the back of the book.

Library of Congress Control Number 2023934881
ISBN 978-0-8307-8568-1
eISBN 978-0-8307-8574-2

The Team: Michael Covington, Kevin Scott,
James Hershberger, Jack Campbell, Susan Murdock
Cover Design: Micah Kandros
Interior Map: Dale Meyers

Printed in the United States of America
First Edition 2023

1 2 3 4 5 6 7 8 9 10

051223

To Trisha:

Your love has given me the gift of being known.
Your grace has given me the safety to be real.
Thank you for choosing me, again.

contents

Justin Davis is my friend. I love him and his family. I have watched his children become adults. He is also an avid fan of the Indianapolis Colts. In a galaxy far, far away, a long, long time ago, that is from 1993–1997, I played professional football for the Indianapolis Colts. Even if I didn't know Justin, though, I *know* his book *Being Real > Being Perfect: How Transparency Leads to Transformation* is going to have an EPIC impact.

Seriously, the Spirit of God is going to operate through Justin's book to heal wounds in your heart that you thought were unhealable. You are reading this book because you want healing. You've come to a place in your life where you are sick and tired of being sick and tired of the person you are pretending to be. As Justin writes, "I learned I could edit my behavior to meet others' expectations without undergoing heart transformation." Justin has and is going through a beautiful transformation because he has learned something that he desperately wants to share with you and me. He's learned that being real > being perfect because Jesus > than us.

Justin is going to walk with you through the valley of the shadow of death, that is the valley of pretending. The valley of pretending is filled with the decaying bones of unrealized dreams, broken promises, lying, adultery, porn addiction, manipulation, and heartbreak. He is going to put your hand in his hand and show you how "to embrace God's preferred picture of you."

When we pretend to not be who God has declared us to be in Christ, we are rejecting God's preferred picture of us (Eph. 1:3–7). When God the Father looks at those who have given their lives and allegiance to His Son, Jesus, through the Spirit's power, these precious ones are now holy, righteous, blameless, perfect, forgiven, and above all, loved beyond measure.

We can stop pretending because we no longer live *for* the approval of people; we now live *from* the approval of God the Father.

We can be transparent because we no longer live *for* the acceptance of others; we now live *from* the acceptance we have in Christ. We can take off the false self because we no longer strive and grind to create an identity based on our achievements; we now live *from* our new identity in Christ based on *His life-giving* achievement, that is His life, death, and resurrection.

You come out of hiding now.

"For you died, and your life is now hidden with Christ in God" (Col. 3:3).

Hiding in His grace,
Derwin Gray
Cofounder and lead pastor of Transformation Church
Author of *The Good Life: What God Teaches about Finding True Happiness*

When I was eight years old, my family lived in a house on a hill with a steep gravel driveway. Water ran down the hill when it rained, making huge, oval mud puddles on each side of the grass-grown median of the driveway. One day, coming home from work, my dad caught me playing in one of those irresistible puddles.

He wasn't as concerned about me playing in the mud as about where those puddles were located—just a few feet from the county road connected to our driveway. My proximity to the road was his biggest concern. His heart was to protect me, but in my mind, he just wanted to keep me from the fun and thrill of playing in the puddle.

My dad had caught me playing in mud puddles before, but until that day, the only consequences had been verbal warnings. This time, though, he didn't say anything; he just took off his belt and whacked me with it several times up the driveway. Depending on your life experience, you may find the physical nature of my dad's disciplinary method appalling. I get it. But this was the early 1980s—before time-outs and grounding children from electronics. I think of it as the "Spare the Rod, Spoil the Child Era" (see Prov. 13:24).

Regardless of your view of corporal punishment, that was the last time I played in a mud puddle. I didn't stop liking mud puddles; I just never wanted to be spanked like that again. That is my first memory of behavior modification.

Over the next twenty years, I became an expert at modifying my behavior to meet others' expectations. I had a specific way I acted at home, at church, on dates, and around friends.

After getting married, I quickly learned what my wife, Trisha, liked and didn't like. I knew what would cause an argument and what would keep the peace. I learned how to deflect questions about sexual purity and pornography. I altered my behavior to avoid conflict.

Being skilled at behavior modification allowed me to compartmentalize my life, marriage, and relationship with God. I learned I could edit my behavior to meet others' expectations without undergoing heart transformation. I believed I could behave my way into a right relationship with God, a healthy marriage, and life-giving relationships. But, man, was I wrong. Relying on behavior modification cost me everything.

In 2013, Trisha and I released our first book, *Beyond Ordinary: When a Good Marriage Just Isn't Good Enough.* The book is a he-said/she-said memoir about how our marriage journeyed, by God's grace, from extraordinary to ordinary to nightmarish and back again. It is a raw, transparent look at the gradual breakdown of our vision of marriage, which eventually led to inauthenticity, deception, sexual brokenness, and infidelity. It's also a story of redemption, healing, and forgiveness, reflected in the most recent seventeen years of our life and marriage.

As Trisha and I have traveled around the country sharing the story of *Beyond Ordinary,* many people have asked "how" questions: How did you change? How did you find transformation? How did you go from broken to healed, addicted to free, bitter to forgiving, dishonest to honest? How are you so open and transparent?

That's similar to a question Christians, especially in the American Church, have been trying to answer for years. How do we change? How do we stop faking it? How do we become the people we are pretending to be? Is it even possible?

More people attend church every Sunday than at any time in history. Every week, songs are sung, prayers are prayed, classes are attended, and sermons are preached and heard. What eludes many followers of Jesus isn't information about God; it's transformation by God. We do all the prescribed Christian behaviors and habits, yet many remain unchanged.

We are conditioned to believe the longer we go to church, the closer to Christ we become. When church attendance and religious activity don't bring heart transformation, though, we often pretend to be closer to God than we are. If we can't transform our hearts, we can at least pretend we're maturing spiritually. We believe:

- We can't let others know we're struggling.
- We can't share our marriage problems with anyone.
- No one can find out about our addictions.
- We can't let anyone know about our strained relationships with our adult kids.
- We can't go to counseling.
- We can't let anyone find out how broken we are.

Over time, we arrive at a place where protecting our reputations seems more important than healing our hearts. We may have major problems or issues. Maybe we have messed up in a significant way. But we refuse to acknowledge it. We pretend it hasn't happened or it's no big deal.

But pretending lust doesn't exist or doesn't cause problems won't solve your lust issues. Faking honesty and transparency won't help you stop lying. Hiding your marriage problems from your family and friends won't keep you from divorce. Being kind in public doesn't resolve the anger you let loose in private. Acting like you have more money than you do won't pay the bills.

Being Real > Being Perfect calls us to let go of the sanitized, inauthentic versions of ourselves and come face to face with the dirty, untouchable parts of our hearts. But we can't stop there. The secret sauce to transformation is when we bring these same broken parts of us into the safety of community with others and the sacredness of our relationship with God. Then we each find the power and grace we need to become someone different, even someone new.

How can we move past pretending for the sake of being real? How can we experience a transformative relationship with God? How can we grow in our knowledge of the Lord and live as authentic followers of Christ? How can we find freedom from public opinion and live to please God?

An authentic life with Jesus isn't easy, but it is possible. Being real over perfect may cost you more than you think you can pay, but it will bring you more than you thought you could have.

This book is a rallying cry for Christians to (1) give up our need to pretend, perform, and be perfect; (2) embrace a real, honest, vulnerable, transparent relationship with Jesus and others; and (3) find the heart transformation we deeply desire.

Let's go on this journey together and discover that being real is more important than being perfect. To experience life change, we will have to assess our desire for authenticity, confront our comfortability with pretending, be willing to give away our shame, and step courageously into our God-given identity.

If you're tired of trying to prove yourself to others and God; if you're over gaining more information about God but not experiencing transformation from God; if you're ready to put down your masks and pretenses to finally live a genuine and authentic life, then this book is for you.

part one

>

a paralyzing predicament

chapter 1

who we pretend to be

authenticity is the path to transformation

> *"To be nobody but yourself in a world which is doing its best day and night*
> *to make you everybody else, means to fight the hardest battle any human*
> *being can fight, and never stop fighting."*
>
> E. E. Cummings, *A Miscellany*

On a cold, snowy morning, my wife, Trisha, and I were sitting in gridlock traffic on I-80 when my phone alerted me to a new message.

Six months earlier, in June 2015, we had moved from Nashville, Tennessee, to Indianapolis, Indiana, to start a new church. Trisha's family was hosting Christmas at their home in Chicago this year. We were slowly making our way there when I received the message that would haunt my life for the next several months.

Trish prefers that I not check messages while driving, so I tried to be inconspicuous as I glanced at my phone. The message was from our new bank:

> Your account's password has been changed. If you did
> not authorize this change, please contact customer ser-
> vice right away.

My heart rate quickened, and my anxiety level skyrocketed. I was confident neither of us had changed our password, so this message was unsettling. I tried to remain calm. *Maybe it's a phishing scheme.*

When traffic slowed again, I opened my bank app and entered my username and password. It responded in RED letters: "Username or password incorrect."

Stealthily, I glanced over at Trish to make sure she hadn't picked up on my phone activity—so far, so good. *Maybe I entered the password incorrectly,* I thought. So I tried again, only to get the same response.

Growing more distressed, I hit my right-turn signal and made my way over to the shoulder. Trish looked up from her iPad and asked, "What's wrong?"

"Did you change the password of the bank account?" I replied, sounding more accusatory than I had intended.

"When?" she asked.

"Like within the past ten minutes?" I said.

"You've been sitting next to me for the last ten minutes," Trish said. "You know I haven't changed the password. What's wrong?"

On the shoulder of the interstate, I put the car in park and turned on the hazard flashers. I closed the bank app and restarted it. I reentered my username and password. Incorrect. I did it again. Incorrect. I tried again and again. Finally, the app responded, "You have entered the incorrect password too many times. Your account is now locked. Please call customer service to reset your password."

I closed the app and tried to log in on the bank website. Same error. I clicked the "Change my password" link and entered my email address. The app said, "No account with that email address is found."

My anxiety was through the roof. I called the bank and began to explain how I had been locked out of my account. After giving the bank representative my Social Security number, she listed the email addresses associated with my account; I recognized none of them. She then asked me to answer the security questions on my account. The answers to those questions had been changed as well.

That was just the beginning. Over the next few weeks, our other bank accounts, our church bank account, the church website, our marriage ministry website, my iCloud account, our email accounts, and my Google account were all hacked. A man who lives in Bangladesh, we now know, had assumed my online identity. Occasionally, he sent me a message asking for money in exchange for returning my accounts to me. Each time I refused to pay, he responded by hacking another account.

Our predator stayed one step ahead of us. He eventually siphoned thousands of dollars out of our bank account, wiped all our computers, and erased our phones. My son texted me from school to tell me his iPad had suddenly locked, went into "Lost Mode," and was erased. There was nothing he could do.

I later learned this guy had hacked into my Dropbox account, where I had a "Master Password" document (not recommended); I also had a copy of my driver's license and PDFs of the tax returns we'd submitted when closing on our house. With those, he had everything he needed to seize every account I owned and also to start new accounts. He opened at least seven new bank accounts in my name.

Over the next three months, I spent fifteen to twenty hours per week working with Apple, Google, my bank, credit-card companies, and even the FBI to recover and reconstruct my online identity.

We closed bank accounts and opened new ones. We regained access to other accounts, one at a time. We made progress in protecting the new accounts we created. One of the biggest challenges was convincing GoDaddy, Google, Apple, and Dropbox that I was the real Justin Davis.

Six months into this ordeal, I received a certified letter from the State Department identifying me as a victim of international cyber terrorism and offering me financial resources to get counseling for any trauma I'd experienced.

Now, to log in to my Gmail account, you have to enter my very encrypted password, as well as a verification code they text to my phone. It's called two-step verification. The same system protects my bank account, iCloud, Facebook, Dropbox, and PayPal accounts.

Based on my experience, the best advice I can offer about passwords is not to use "jordan," "Jordan," "jordan23," "Jordan23," "jordan#23," or "Jordan#23" as your password for every online account you own. Apply that wisdom, and you should be pretty safe.

If it's not already apparent, this went way beyond passwords and online accounts. My entire life had been hacked, and someone was pretending to be me. A fake Justin Davis was doing real damage to my family and me, threatening the quality of our future.

One afternoon, I hit my lowest low on the phone with a very kind and patient woman from Apple. At one point, I declared emphatically, "I promise you I am the real Justin Davis!" She said, "I want to believe you, but I have no way of knowing if you are the real Justin Davis."

I wish this were the only time I'd lost my identity. Unfortunately, I have forfeited it repeatedly, each time pretending to be someone I was not. I wish the guy in Bangladesh were the only fake version of me. But the truth is that I was in the habit of creating bogus versions of myself for years. Those fake versions of me hijacked relationships, robbed me of intimacy with God, and threatened the quality of my future.

Some of my biggest regrets in life are the moments lost and the relationships I wounded by pretending to be someone other than who God created me to be. My guess is that you have some fake versions of you out there too. You have a version of you that you present at work; another at church; even another for your in-laws. Even if you don't have a guy in Bangladesh pretending to be you (and I hope you don't), you create fake versions of you every day.

I imagine, if asked, that you'd say you value authenticity. You are probably drawn to people who are genuine and honest, and you want that for yourself. But in the quietness of your heart, you know that parts of you are fake and inauthentic.

You are not alone.

the impostor

In his book *Abba's Child*, Brennan Manning talked about our capacity to pretend by creating "impostors." Manning said we create impostors out of insecurity, fear, or pain, where the best versions of ourselves are who we pretend to be. He wrote:

> When I was eight, the impostor, or false self, was born as a defense against pain. The impostor within whispered, "Brennan, don't ever be your real self anymore because nobody likes you as you are. Invent a new self that everybody will admire and nobody will know. So I became a good boy—polite, well mannered, unobtrusive, and deferential. I studied hard, scored excellent grades, won a scholarship in high school, and was stalked every

waking moment by the terror of abandonment and the
sense that nobody was there for me. I learned that perfect performance brought the recognition and approval I
desperately sought.[1]

God created you with a unique identity. I'm not talking about a Social
Security number, fingerprint, or retina scan. I'm talking about a God-
given, image-bearing identity that gives you value and purpose and sets
you apart for God's glory. Yet we often lose that identity and settle for a
counterfeit version over who we were created to be. Why do so many God-
loving, churchgoing, worship-song-singing Christians choose to pretend
over being real?

who we think we should be

For many of us, there is a gap between who we are and who we think we
should be. That gap is defined by one word: *should*. You should be a better
mom. You should be a better husband. You should be more fit. You should
be further along in your career. You should be more spiritually mature. You
should be more financially secure at your age. You should be more prepared
for retirement. You should be a better friend. Our list of "shoulds" grows as
our responsibilities in life increase. When the gap becomes too wide, we
concede who we are and fake our way into who we should be.

In 2005, I started a job as a headhunter, placing commercial bankers in
banks in Chicago and Indianapolis. It was an over-the-phone sales job. Pre-
viously, I was a pastor for ten years and never had a job outside the church. I
had no idea what I was doing.

Successful headhunter strategy involves calling companies to discover
what job openings they need help filling. Then, you convince them you are

the person to find the talent they desire. Next, you get them to sign an agreement that they will pay you a fee if they hire a candidate you present. After that, you try to find a candidate with the skills and experience required for the position. If they are willing to consider a new opportunity at this new company, you prepare them for the interview process, work with the company's human resources staff to coordinate interviews, negotiate the offer with both the company and the candidate, walk the candidate through the process of resigning their old job, and educate them on the dangers of accepting a counteroffer from their current employer. With all that time invested, you cross your fingers and pray that they will pass the background check and drug test and show up on their first day of work. Finally, thirty days after their start date, you get paid.

I have a Christian Education degree from a small Bible college in central Illinois. I had no clue what a headhunter was until I became a headhunter. My boss was a seasoned veteran in the headhunting business, so he helped me develop a script I could use for phone calls. The script was terrific for all the voice mails I left for people who didn't answer their phones. But on my second day, a person answered the phone. He was a human resources person at a bank in Aurora, Illinois. I introduced myself and went through my script. He wasn't impressed. He asked me a few questions about previous positions I'd filled (there were none), other banks I'd worked with (again, none), what size portfolios most of the commercial lenders I worked with carried (I hadn't worked with any commercial lenders), what was their average fee income (what is fee income?), and what were their annual deposits (what?). If you are confused by this terminology, that is precisely where I was. But I had to convince him I was an expert.

So, I started regurgitating terms and words I'd heard him say and restated some of the comments I'd made in my opening script. Silence. Then he said, "How long have you been doing this?" I said, "Today is my second day. I'm just trying to fake it till I make it." He said, "Well, that's a strategy. How's it working for you?" It wasn't.

Faking it till you make it is sometimes essential; you have to start somewhere. But when it becomes a spiritual strategy, we begin to lose our God-given identity and purpose. We become driven by what we should do or who we should impress, rather than who God created us to be. When our fear of not being enough causes us to pretend we have it all together, we lose our ability to experience transformation.

Fake your joy.

Fake your contentment.

Fake your spiritual life.

Fake your financial peace.

Fake your relational health.

Fake your marital happiness.

The problem for many of us is that we become experts at faking it but never make it. So, we keep faking.

who we think God wants us to be

I grew up in the church. My parents came to faith when I was a baby. By the time I was in elementary school, they were heavily involved in our small congregation. We were at church every time the doors were open. Sunday morning, Sunday night, and Wednesday night were built into our family rhythm. Yet as I think back on my early experience in the church, I can't remember one sermon on God's love or His grace or compassion. Instead, I recall several sermons on God's laws, commands, and expectations.

The reason I came into a relationship with Jesus wasn't a desire to have a relationship with the God of the universe through the person of Jesus Christ. I accepted Christ because I didn't want to go to hell.

When I was ten years old, I went to a church camp. The speaker that week was a fire-and-brimstone type of preacher. I remember the temperature outside on the last night of camp was superhot. All the campers and counselors had squeezed into this small non-air-conditioned chapel. I recall the preacher leaning over the massive pulpit on the stage and saying, "If you think this is hot, you've not felt anything yet. Hell is hotter. If you don't want to go to hell and burn for all of eternity, then you need to accept Jesus Christ as your personal Savior tonight!" Spit was flying from his mouth, as his finger pointed out to the audience. I felt as though his gaze had caught me, and his finger was pointing down into the depths of my soul. My hand went up. I walked the aisle. I repented of my previous ten years of lawlessness and sin. I committed my life to Jesus.

That "conversion" experience shaped my spiritual life over the next twenty years. I didn't think of God as a heavenly Father who wanted to have a relationship with me, a son of the King. I thought of Him as an angry judge that tried to make me into a dutiful servant. I didn't think of myself as a follower of Jesus but as a follower of rules. Spiritual growth wasn't measured by how much I became like Christ but by how good and faithful I could be, and how much I served and sacrificed. It was a relationship built on obligation and fear, not gratitude and grace.

> The reason I accepted Christ was because I didn't want to go to hell.

Author John Ortberg said, "There is an enormous difference between following rules and following Jesus."[2] I was doing my best to follow rules and equating it with following Jesus.

When you and I come to the end of our ability to live up to God's rules and standards and realize we can never be good enough to be who we think God wants us to be, our natural reflex is to pretend to be what we believe God wants. We are not marked by authentic transformation but by incremental behavior modification topped off with an inauthentic spirituality.

who we want others to believe we are

Regardless of where we grow up—in the country, inner city, or suburbia—we live with a constant battle to portray our lives to others in a certain way. Maybe for you it's a stable career and a nice car. Or perhaps it's being a stay-at-home mom with a nice side-hustle income, or the urban farmer who lives the ultimate farm-to-table lifestyle.

We acquire an idea of what success looks like, then go to great lengths to achieve it. However, as the need to be successful grows, so does our insecurity over missing out on that success. We don't fear failure as much as we fear others receiving us as a failure. That fear causes insecurity.

Insecurity tells us there is only one path. To be successful, you need to have _____ and be _____ (you fill in the blanks). Insecurity says you're not enough, so you strive to be more and, in doing so, feel defeated in who you have or haven't become.

As culture marks a path for who we should be, our faith system tells us how to act along the way. Becoming who people want you to be is more valuable than being your authentic self.

Social media has been a game changer in shaping our culture. It's also become a powerful force in shaping our hearts. No longer are we only being shaped by our immediate surroundings of people we physically interact with daily. Social media, for better or worse, has broadened how we are influenced and influence others. Amid this culture-shaping shift, social media doubles down on the pressure we feel to live up to others' expectations or perceptions of us.

We read blogs, tweets, and Instagram posts and fight a battle of celebrating and envying the content we are consuming. But I think our struggle has less to do with envying the lives of others and more with our natural inclination to compare our lives to those we scroll past online—and how that causes us to redefine how we see ourselves.

When culture and faith collide, it has the power to create profound change. For many of us, the collision leaves us depressed when we're not accepted. Although, as Christians, we share the same Jesus, our views of what it means to live a Jesus-centered life are vastly different. Opinions, debates, and arguments brew over what it means to be a follower of Christ; a gap is created between the person you feel called to be and the person you think others want or perceive you to be. In that tension, we settle for living an inauthentic life.

lessons from 1 Samuel

The book of 1 Samuel tells a story of culture and faith colliding. For hundreds of years, the people of Israel were governed and led by a judge who was appointed by God and had the Spirit of the Lord with him to help guide and shape the hearts of the Israelites. Samuel was faithful to God, leading the Israelites to many victories against the nation's enemies. As he neared retirement, Samuel appointed his sons, Joel and Abijah, to judge Israel. Unfortunately, rather than following in their father's footsteps, they were both corrupt leaders, and the people revolted.

even so, even though

Then, the people of Israel took notice of the pagan communities prospering under the leadership of a king. They shifted their focus to a cultural definition of success, instead of trusting God's plan. They complained to Samuel to ask God to give them a king instead of more judges. God agreed to their request but gave them this warning:

> So Samuel passed on the LORD's warning to the people who were asking him for a king. "This is how a king will reign over you," Samuel said. "The king will draft your sons and assign them to his chariots and his charioteers, making them run before his chariots. Some will be generals and captains in his army, some will be forced to plow in his fields and harvest his crops, and some will make his weapons and chariot equipment. The king will take your daughters from you and force them to cook and bake and make perfumes for him. He will take away the best of your fields and vineyards and olive groves and give them to his own officials. He will take a tenth of your grain and your grape harvest and distribute it among his officers and attendants. He will take your male and female slaves and demand the finest of your cattle and donkeys for his own use. He will demand a tenth of your flocks, and you will be his slaves. When that day comes, you will beg for relief from this king you are demanding, but then the LORD will not help you."
>
> But the people refused to listen to Samuel's warning. "Even so, we still want a king," they said. "We want to be

like the nations around us. Our king will judge us and
lead us into battle."

So Samuel repeated to the LORD what the people
had said, and the LORD replied, "Do as they say, and give
them a king." Then Samuel agreed and sent the people
home. (1 Sam. 8:10–22 NLT)

Notice their response to the warning: "Even so, we still want a king."
Even so, they received their king and the cultural acceptance they desired,
while forfeiting their true identity as a holy nation. "Even so" transitions to
"even though."

Even though God clearly warned them of the consequences, their desire
to fit into their culture trumped their desire to follow God's plan. Unfortunately, we allow the same thing to happen in our lives. It's the entryway to
inauthenticity.

Even though you know your dating relationship isn't healthy, you can't
imagine anyone better loving you. Rather than trusting God with your dating life, you settle.

Even though your credit cards are maxed out, and you're struggling
financially, you see your possessions as indications of your value, so you keep
charging and buying.

Even though your spouse has asked you to find a job that requires less
travel so you can be home more, your identity is wrapped up in the thrill of
the sale.

Even though we know the life God calls us to is not the life we pretend
to have, we keep faking it. As a result, we forfeit our identity and forgo
transformation.

The life you desire isn't about how successful or how popular you can become. Nor is it about living a perfect, flawless life in the eyes of others. Living an authentic relationship with God is about living a life transformed by Him.

overlooked and forgotten

As we continue in the book of 1 Samuel, we come to the end of Saul's reign as king of Israel and God's desire to anoint a new king. The prophet Samuel was sent to the house of Jesse to find and anoint the new king from among Jesse's eight sons.

In a ceremony almost as dramatic as *The Bachelor*, Jesse lined up each of his sons for Samuel to evaluate and determine which one was most worthy of being king of Israel. The seven sons stood in a line from oldest to youngest, each ready to confidently present himself as the obvious choice to be the next king of Israel.

Samuel went down the line, but God didn't confirm any of the sons. Samuel then asked if this was all of Jesse's sons. "'There is still the youngest,' Jesse replied. 'But he is out in the fields watching the sheep and goats'" (1 Sam. 16:11 NLT).

As a dad, I believe my kids are more talented, more intelligent, better looking, more deserving of playing time, and more likely to be the teacher's favorite and become popular than any other kid on the planet. I think my kids are amazing.

Jesse thought that of his seven sons. But when it came to David and the opportunity to be considered king of Israel, Jesse didn't even invite him to the ceremony. David's dad didn't even think to bring him in from tending sheep.

Imagine the scene. This was a huge family moment. So much planning and preparation went into a ceremony like this. This event changed the destiny of Jesse's family forever, and David wasn't even asked to come in from the field. He was not invited. Do you think David had daddy wounds?

taking off the ill-fitting armor

In 1 Samuel 17, the shepherd boy David was asked to run an errand for his father. David's older brothers were at war with the Philistines, and they had forgotten to pack a lunch. So Jesse asked David to take them something to eat.

When David arrived on the battlefield, there was no battle. It was a standoff. The Philistines had a giant, and Saul, the king of Israel, believed they had no hope.

We pick up the story:

> "Don't worry about this Philistine," David told Saul. "I'll go fight him!"
>
> "Don't be ridiculous!" Saul replied. "There's no way you can fight this Philistine and possibly win! You're only a boy, and he's been a man of war since his youth."
>
> But David persisted. "I have been taking care of my father's sheep and goats," he said. "When a lion or a bear comes to steal a lamb from the flock, I go after it with a club and rescue the lamb from its mouth. If the animal turns on me, I catch it by the jaw and club it to death. I have done this to both lions and bears, and I'll do it to this pagan Philistine, too, for he has defied the armies of the

living God! The LORD who rescued me from the claws of the lion and the bear will rescue me from this Philistine!"

Saul finally consented. "All right, go ahead," he said. "And may the LORD be with you!"

Then Saul gave David his own armor—a bronze helmet and a coat of mail. David put it on, strapped the sword over it, and took a step or two to see what it was like, for he had never worn such things before.

"I can't go in these," he protested to Saul. "I'm not used to them." So David took them off again. (1 Sam. 17:32–39 NLT)

So he took them off.

David wasn't invited to the king's anointing ceremony. His father forgot him. David wasn't as physically mature or impressive as his seven brothers. Yet at this moment, he said, "I know who I am, and I can't be me wearing your armor." David had confident security in his identity. It is remarkable that in this defining moment, David was so secure in who he was—and more importantly, in what God had called him to do—that he had no compulsion to fake it till he made it.

So he took them off.

> God can change who you are.
> What God can't do is make you
> into who you pretend to be.

You are in a battle too. I love this quote from E. E. Cummings so much, I want you to read it again:

> To be nobody but yourself in a world which is doing its best day and night to make you everybody else, means to fight the hardest battle any human being can fight, and never stop fighting.[3]

God sees you. He has chosen you and given you an identity. You don't have to wear someone else's armor to be impressive to God.

Here is my question to you as we start this journey together: What do you need to take off to start being you and stop being who you are pretending to be?

> Take off pretending to have it more together than you do.
>
> Take off acting like your marriage is better than it is.
>
> Take off portraying that your addiction doesn't have control over you.
>
> Take off faking you are closer to God than you are.
>
> Take off make-believing you have more money than you do.

We all want to change. We all want to be different. If change and transformation were based on desire, we'd all be twenty pounds lighter, have more money in the bank, and have no relationship issues. Changes are based on choices. The best choice you can make today is to take off the expectations of others, take off your perception of who God wants you to be, take off the "shoulds" you are placing on yourself.

Take them off. They don't fit.

Justin, you don't know how broken I am. No, but God does, and He loves you in your brokenness. *Justin, you don't see how messed up my marriage is.* No, but God is fighting for your marriage even more than you are. *Justin, you don't know how dysfunctional my dating life is.* No, but God specializes in bringing healing from dysfunction. *Justin, you don't know how numb I feel spiritually.* No, but admitting your distance from God is the first step in finding your way back to Him.

God can change who you are. What God can't do is make you into who you pretend to be. God can only transform the parts of your heart you are willing to give to Him.

Authenticity is the pathway to the transformation you desperately desire.

chapter 2

do we really want authenticity?

authenticity is the cry of many but the game of few

> "Authenticity is the daily practice of letting go of who we think we're supposed to be and embracing who we are."
>
> Brené Brown, *The Gifts of Imperfection*

A few months ago, my nineteen-year-old son, Isaiah, hit the pause button on all his social media apps. Through a series of events and conversations, the presence of social media in his life had robbed him of being present with God and others. So, he deleted Snapchat, deactivated his Instagram account, and signed out of Twitter. It was a bold move for someone a month away from graduating high school, but he felt like it was the right thing for him.

The following week, we were out to dinner as a family to celebrate my birthday, and I saw him take a selfie and noticed his phone's screen flash as he posed. I said, "I thought you were off of social media." As the words came out of my mouth, I felt myself channeling my dad's tone of voice when he disapproved of something. I intended to be inquisitive, but instead, I made it sound like an inquisition.

Isaiah said, "This is a different kind of app—it's called BeReal."

"What is BeReal?" I asked. (I might as well have said, "I'm old.")

He explained that most of his friends had transitioned to this newer app, which is the opposite of Instagram. "Instead of sharing the highlight reel of your life on Instagram, BeReal captures real life. You get a notification from a friend and have two minutes to take a picture and share it. There are no filters, and you can't edit it. It's the real you. When you take a picture on the front camera, it also takes a picture from the back camera. So your friends see the real you and where you are in that moment. It encourages everyone to be real and present. My friends are kinda tired of the fake versions of everyone."

I'd never heard of BeReal, so I did some research. In April 2022, an article in *Social Media Today* said this about the app:

> BeReal, as the name suggests, is focused on real, authentic connection, an un-edited view on social sharing, designed to help people take a step away from the overly curated feeds of other apps.[1]

At the time the article was written, the app had been downloaded 7.4 million times, and its download rate was up 315 percent in 2022. Fifty-five percent of BeReal users were Gen Z in the age-group of 16 to 24, and 43 percent were in the 25 to 44 range. In an August 2022 article, *Time* reported that BeReal's global users had grown to 22.8 million.[2]

The app is "designed to help people take a step away from the overly curated feeds." As a culture, we're used to photoshopped pictures, filtered social media posts, curated timelines, and photo grids that enhance our brand, style, or reputation. Being real is so unexpected it's refreshing.

Merriam-Webster's Dictionary has a few definitions of the word *authentic*, but two stick out to me:

- "Not false or imitation"
- "True to one's own personality, spirit, or character"

Used in a sentence, *Merriam-Webster's* says, *"Authentic* means being actually and exactly what is claimed."[3]

I have an interactive exercise for you while you read this paragraph. Are you ready? As you continue reading, see if you've inherited the genetic ability to roll your tongue. If you can, you are part of at least 65 percent of the world's population who can roll their tongues, according to a BBC article.[4]

What does tongue-rolling have to do with authenticity? While you may have inherited the ability to roll your tongue, it still takes practice to do it on command. Also, people not genetically inclined to roll their tongues can learn to do it with enough practice.

While not a genetic ability, authenticity is a character trait you can grow into with enough effort. No matter how real or fake you are right now, you can start where you are and continue the journey to becoming the most authentic version of yourself.

Each year, during the week between Christmas and New Year's, our family sets goals for the upcoming year. First, we review the goals from the previous year, and then we set new goals. It's now a running joke that, for the last X years, my goal has been to "lose 40 pounds." As we were setting goals last December, my son said, "Let me guess, Dad: your number one goal for next year is to lose 40 pounds." Another chimed in, "He should have lost 160 pounds by now if he'd hit his 40-pound goal each year." Whatever.

Like getting in shape, authentic living starts with a decision, then becomes a process and, ultimately, a way of living. It can't be a onetime decision or a stated goal. If you want to be authentic, you have to make repeated, daily decisions to peel back layers of veneer you've used to polish your reputation, image, and character.

Being "exactly what is claimed" is a choice you have to make in small and big ways that add up over time to being real.

Proverbs 11:3 says, "The integrity of the upright guides them, but the unfaithful are destroyed by their duplicity." If authenticity is defined by being true to one's character, inauthenticity could be summarized by the word *duplicity*. Proverbs says that duplicity—not being real, honest, or authentic—will keep you from having the life you desire. Duplicity actively destroys God's best for you.

According to *Merriam-Webster's*, the idea of doubleness is at the root of duplicity. "*Duplicity* comes from a Latin word meaning 'double' or 'twofold,' and its original meaning in English has to do with a kind of deception in which you intentionally hide your true feelings or intentions behind false words or actions." It can also mean "double vision" or "seeing double."[5]

The idea is that there are two of you—the one you're showing and the one you're hiding. Duplicity is hiding a part of you to make people believe something that's not true.

conditioned for duplicity

As authenticity is a process, duplicity or inauthenticity is also a learned process. Developing either of these stems from the everyday needs we all have from birth.

Abraham Maslow was an American psychologist best known for creating a "hierarchy of needs," a theory of psychological health predicated on fulfilling innate human needs. His theory was first published in 1943, and since that time, many psychologists have added to and modified it. But everyone agrees with the three basic human needs on Maslow's list:

- Safety/Survival
- Love/Acceptance
- Identity/Significance

There is no debate about these needs. Each and every one of us needs all three.

In addition to these innate needs, many people and circumstances influence us to choose authenticity or duplicity. For example, some relational ecosystems, at first glance, you might think are full of authenticity. But the environments or relationships in which we long to be our most authentic selves are often those in which we are most conditioned to be duplicitous.

family

Your family unit should be where you feel most comfortable and safe being authentic. Unfortunately, that's not the case for most of us. If your family is anything like mine, you first learned duplicity within your family.

Family units function best when we are confident our basic human needs will be met there. Safety, love, and identity are the foundation of healthy families. Would it surprise you to hear that most American families struggle to fulfill these three basic human needs? Families can be places of great love, but they can also be places of great pain. We learn to manage that pain and project a more positive image of our family to those outside our family. Here are a few key stats about the average American family:

- Thirty percent of the children in the United States, according to the 2022 Census, have divorced parents.[6]
- One in four girls and one in thirteen boys have been sexually abused. Ninety-one percent of those sexually abused were victimized by a friend or family member.[7]
- Forty-six percent of US adults reported having dealt with substance abuse in their families.[8]

Family dysfunction isn't just in our time. Look at the families in the Old Testament. From the fall of humanity to today, families have struggled to be a place of safety and acceptance.

school

When I was ten years old, my family moved from a farmhouse just outside Ladoga, Indiana, a town of around eight hundred people, to Crawfordsville, Indiana, a city of sixteen thousand, about twenty miles away.

Until our move, I had never recognized the differences in social status and income brackets. We were very poor. We shopped for school clothes at yard sales, were often on food stamps, and routinely borrowed money from my grandparents to cover unexpected expenses. My dad often worked two or three jobs to pay our bills, but that was normal.

When we arrived in Crawfordsville that summer, our poverty became obvious to me. I realized how poor we were financially and how needy I was relationally. I did not fit in. At all.

I wore yard-sale Wrangler jeans, and the kids in Crawfordsville wore Guess jeans. I had weather-worn vinyl cowboy boots, and the popular kids just got the newly invented Nike Air Jordans. I rode a Huffy bicycle my dad got from my cousin; the cool kids rode high-end off-road bicycles called Redlines. I wore generic T-shirts spotted with holes and stains, and the kids I wanted to be friends with wore Izod shirts emblazoned with the alligator logo sewn on the left pocket.

I have no good memories of that transition, only memories of being bullied and ostracized. I was made fun of so often that I developed a stomach condition that I assume now were ulcers from feeling anxious about going to school and facing kids I didn't fit in with. I desperately wanted my life to be different.

Shortly after we moved, I got a paper route to begin earning my own money. My parents couldn't afford the lifestyle I thought would bring me acceptance, so I saved my money to buy the Air Jordans, Guess jeans, and Izod shirts. It would take me years to realize that wearing the right clothes or riding a high-end bike wouldn't give me the acceptance I needed.

The desire to be popular, at its core, is the essential need to find acceptance. Popularity isn't always determined by personality, sense of humor, or character. Many times it's based on the family you're born into, the connections your parents have, or the tax bracket you fit into. Popularity whispers, "Do whatever you have to do to fit in."

The currency of popularity is often conformity at the cost of authenticity. So many people I know experienced the same thing throughout their school-age years: everyone trying to be more like other people rather than feeling comfortable being themselves.

church

I wish I could say that the American Church is a safe place to be real and authentic, but for many, that isn't the case. The Church has become a place to hide, not be known. We've curated church cultures that only show the best versions of ourselves while hiding the real us.

My parents were married for thirty-six years before getting divorced. I'll share more about this later in the book, but my dad had a secret life full of sexual sin and hiddenness that came to light and ended their marriage. Growing up, I knew my parents didn't have a great marriage. They didn't argue all the time, just when they were together. (I say that kind of sarcastically.) My dad worked six days a week, so Sunday was the only day we were all together. On Sundays, we went to church, no questions asked, and I recall several times when my parents got into arguments on the way to services. Many of their arguments were volatile, loud, and even physical.

One of the biggest pre-church arguments I remember happened the morning church-directory pictures were to be taken. Are you old enough to remember church-directory pictures? If not, think "yearbook pictures for church." We were scheduled to have our family picture taken during the Sunday-school hour that preceded the worship service. My parents got into an all-time argument. I have three younger siblings, and the louder my parents yelled at each other, the harder and louder my siblings and I cried. By the time we made it to the church, all six of us were crying; we were a mess. Tears were streaming, snot flowing, eyes puffy and red. My dad was intimidating and controlling. He pulled into a parking space at the back of the lot so we'd have a long way to walk. After parking, he looked in the back seat and said, "We're at church. Everyone dry it up, and get over it. It's time to take our family picture and worship the Lord. Dry it up. If you can't dry it up, then stay in the car."

Message sent loud and clear—the Church isn't a place for your drama. Church isn't a place for your mess. Dry it up. Suck it up. Fake it.

We want to be real and authentic, but our desire for authenticity is often greater than our commitment to it.

Why do we struggle with authenticity? For many of us, we equate vulnerability with weakness. We associate authenticity with being needy. We think of being authentic as being dramatic or high maintenance. There is no doubt that, in our social media culture, we are bombarded with people who are too honest, transparent, and drama filled. They use drama, crisis, and catastrophe to share publicly what should only be shared in the context of a friendship or relationship.

But authenticity always starts privately before it's seen publicly. While we may equate the small-group oversharer or the Facebook broadcaster with authenticity, that is *counterfeit* authenticity. That is a vulnerability for the sake of pity, attention, or both—not transformation.

> Authenticity always starts privately before it's seen publicly.

I love what researcher Brené Brown said in her book *Daring Greatly*, "Vulnerability sounds like truth and feels like courage. Truth and courage aren't always comfortable, but they're never weakness."[9]

the DNA of transformation

Authenticity takes self-awareness, humility, courage, and commitment. It's a process we enter and continue to grow into, not a destination to which we arrive. How we respond to the call of authenticity determines the depth of life transformation we experience.

In John 4, Jesus encountered a woman who had lived in duplicity and hiddenness for years. Then, she met Jesus, and everything changed—through an offer of authenticity. Let's set up the scene, look at this encounter, and see how the DNA of transformation came alive.

> Now Jesus learned that the Pharisees had heard that he was gaining and baptizing more disciples than John— although in fact it was not Jesus who baptized, but his disciples. So he left Judea and went back once more to Galilee. (John 4:1–3)

I included the first three verses in this passage specifically for verse 3, "So he left Judea and went back once more to Galilee." Galilee was in the northern region of Israel; Judea the southern. The area between Galilee and Judea was a place called Samaria. The Jewish people hated Samaria and its people. Likewise, the Samaritans despised the Jews.

This was a historical hatred that spanned generations. Samaritans were Jewish people who intermarried with the Assyrians after the Assyrian conquest of Israel in approximately 721 BC. Since they were not of "pure Jewish descent," the Jewish people wouldn't allow them into their synagogues, wouldn't allow them to become citizens, and avoided any social interaction with them. The Jews considered them to be far from God and not a part of God's chosen people.

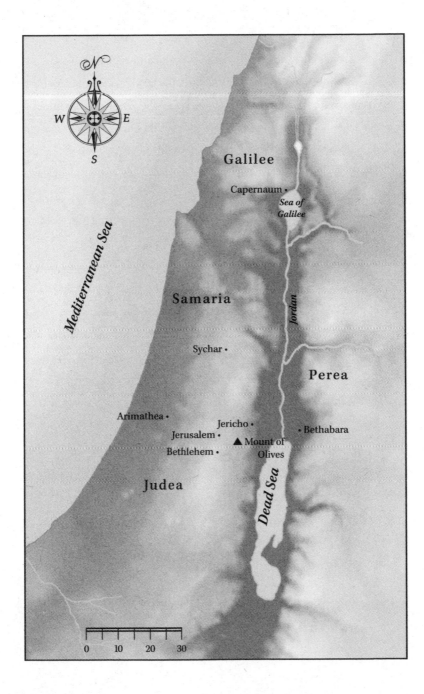

The journey between Galilee and Judea was familiar to the Jewish people. It was about eighty miles between the two locations. Scholars estimate a three- to four-day journey from one place to the other in that time. But the Jewish people hated the Samaritans so much that they refused to go directly from one location to the other because they would have to cross through Samaria. Instead, the Jewish people went around Samaria, crossed the Jordan River twice, and added two to three days to their trip—all to avoid going through Samaria.

This context makes verse 4 very compelling: "Now he had to go through Samaria" (John 4:4).

We don't know why Jesus had to go through Samaria. John didn't tell us. We only know that this place every religious leader and rabbi avoided was the very place Jesus had to go. This was a divine appointment.

There are places in our hearts that we try to avoid at all costs. We have a place where we store regrets, mistakes, shame, and guilt. We have addictions, habits, impure thoughts, and sinful choices we try to keep in the Samaria of our hearts. We believe life is best lived by not going to that place. If we can distance ourselves from those choices, mistakes, wounds, abuses, and sins, we may live up to God's standards and expectations. There is no way God would want anything to do with the things that live in our Samaria.

"He had to go through Samaria."

Today is your divine appointment.

Now let's look at some of the components of the DNA of authenticity.

self-awareness

So he came to a town in Samaria called Sychar, near the plot of ground Jacob had given to his son Joseph. Jacob's

well was there, and Jesus, tired as he was from the journey, sat down by the well. It was about noon.

When a Samaritan woman came to draw water,
Jesus said to her, "Will you give me a drink?" (His disciples had gone into the town to buy food.)

The Samaritan woman said to him, "You are a Jew
and I am a Samaritan woman. How can you ask me for
a drink?" (For Jews do not associate with Samaritans.)
(John 4:5–9)

These verses show the most crucial component of the DNA of authenticity: self-awareness. God can't change the things we won't acknowledge.
The Samaritan woman addressed two things that, at the time, were seen as
weaknesses—her gender and her race: "You are a Jew and I am a Samaritan
woman."

We don't even know this woman's name. But she knew that Jesus
should not be talking to her. A Jewish rabbi would never publicly address
a woman, especially a Samaritan woman. She was shocked. Verse 27
describes the disciples' surprise to find Jesus talking to a Samaritan
woman. Jesus was making a statement: Transformation is for everyone.
Jesus is for everyone.

If you want to be an authentic person, the first step is self-awareness.
You can't get out of debt until you know how far you are in debt. You can't
lose weight until you know how much you want to lose. Defining reality is
the first step in transforming your reality.

In 2005, my wife, Trish, and I separated because of my affair. The damage
this did to my wife and kids, friends, family, and church family is impossible
to quantify. We were separated for two and a half months and started going

to counseling. In one of our first sessions, our counselor told us that, while the affair was hurtful and damaging, it was also a symptom of deeper issues in our lives and marriage. To find authentic healing, we'd have to dig below the hurt of the affair and address those things.

Thirty days into our counseling, I confessed to Trish and our counselor that I'd been sexually abused and struggled with pornography. This was another bombshell I dropped on Trish, just at a point when we'd started to find some healing. It was so hurtful and such a considerable setback that our counselor suggested he meet with us individually for the next few sessions.

The next day, I showed up at my appointment and started talking about my ten-year struggle with pornography. After a few minutes, my counselor interrupted me and said, "You keep referring to your relationship with porn by saying, 'I struggle.' What does that mean?"

I said, "It means that I'm not a porn addict or anything. I just struggle."

He sat back in his chair. "How many times did you say you would never look at porn again?" he asked.

"Every time," I said.

"How long did that promise last?" he replied.

"It lasted until the next time. Sometimes that was a day, a week, a month. It varied." I thought I was building an excellent case for my use of the word *struggle*.

"So, you promise yourself and God that you will never look at porn again. And you keep that promise until you can't keep that promise anymore, and you look at porn again, and again, and again. Would you say that you were controlling it, or it was controlling you?"

I hadn't thought about it that way. "I guess it was controlling me," I said reluctantly.

"So if it was controlling you, that isn't a struggle; that is an addiction. You can't find freedom from addiction until you are willing to admit you have one."

A lack of self-awareness usually means the presence of self-deception. It's not that we're unaware of the things that need to be transformed in our lives; we are unwilling to tell ourselves the truth about them.

Self-deception is the greatest deception because everything we do is filtered through our inability or unwillingness to tell ourselves the truth. Once we are open to self-awareness, it leads to the next component of the DNA of authenticity.

humility

Jesus answered her, "If you knew the gift of God and who it is that asks you for a drink, you would have asked him and he would have given you living water."

"Sir," the woman said, "you have nothing to draw with and the well is deep. Where can you get this living water? Are you greater than our father Jacob, who gave us the well and drank from it himself, as did also his sons and his livestock?"

Jesus answered, "Everyone who drinks this water will be thirsty again, but whoever drinks the water I give them will never thirst. Indeed, the water I give them will become in them a spring of water welling up to eternal life."

The woman said to him, "Sir, give me this water so that I won't get thirsty and have to keep coming here to draw water." (John 4:10–15)

Humility can be described and defined in many ways. *Merriam-Webster's* defines it as "freedom from pride or arrogance."[10]

Rick Warren, author of *The Purpose-Driven Life*, described humility by saying, "Humility isn't thinking less of yourself; it's thinking of yourself less."[11]

Humility is hard to quantify, no matter how you define or describe it. But when someone has it, you know—and when they don't, you know.

For our purposes, humility is a willingness to admit you lack something and are willing to ask for it. Remember, the spiritual conversation between Jesus and the woman had been pretty one sided. The woman had come to the well to draw water, and upon encountering Jesus, she realized He had something she didn't know she needed.

To her, at that moment, Jesus was the equivalent of Apple or Costco. Steve Jobs was known for creating products we didn't think we needed. Costco is the same way for me. I went to Costco to buy milk and eggs and didn't realize I needed a twelve-man tent, a fourteen-burner outdoor kitchen, and a three-year supply of vitamins. The woman came to the well to get water for the day and realized there was water that could quench her thirst for all time. Unfortunately, she didn't have it, but she was willing to ask Jesus for it. That's humility.

Humility, in the process of being authentic, says, "I know I tend to hide. I recognize my default response to be less than honest. I see the impostors I create in various aspects of my life, and I need help. I need something different. I need something from You, Jesus, that I don't have."

"Sir, give me this water so I won't get thirsty and have to keep coming here to draw water."

What do you need from Jesus? Are you willing to humble yourself and admit you need help? You need help with your temper, control issues, dishonesty, drinking, looking to accomplishments for value, addiction, or way of looking for and expressing love. You need something from Jesus that you don't have. Otherwise, you return to the well only to receive the same non-transformative water.

courage

> He told her, "Go, call your husband and come back."
>
> "I have no husband," she replied.
>
> Jesus said to her, "You are right when you say you have no husband. The fact is, you have had five husbands, and the man you now have is not your husband. What you have just said is quite true."
>
> "Sir," the woman said, "I can see that you are a prophet. Our ancestors worshiped on this mountain, but you Jews claim that the place where we must worship is in Jerusalem." …
>
> The woman said, "I know that Messiah" (called Christ) "is coming. When he comes, he will explain everything to us."
>
> Then Jesus declared, "I, the one speaking to you—I am he." (John 4:16–20, 25–26)

This conversation went unexpectedly and uncomfortably deep very fast. Jesus and the Samaritan woman went from talking about thirst, water, and genealogy to marriage, failed relationships, moral choices, and the sin, shame, and brokenness she carried to the well.

In that culture, women gathered water daily for the family's needs. It was customary for the women to go to the well early, around 6:00 a.m. They drew what they needed for the day and then escaped the day's heat. This woman was at the well at noon on purpose.

Noon was the hottest part of the day. No one went to the well in the middle of the day to get water, unless they felt they had no other choice. This woman knew her past, and everyone in the community knew her history. She came at noon because she was trying to avoid people, not go deep with people—especially a Jewish rabbi.

How do you react when you are confronted? How do you respond when someone shines a light on your sin?

One of the things we tell our kids is, "Defensiveness is the first sign of guilt." If I tell one of my kids, "Let me see your phone." And their response is, "What do you need my phone for? Why do you need my phone?" We have a problem.

This woman's deepest wounds, biggest regrets, and most embarrassing sins were exposed in the middle of the day by a Jewish man who had just revealed himself as the Savior of the world. She could have left her bucket at the well and walked away. She could have denied her reality and tried to lie her way out of it. She could have come back at Jesus, "What right do you have to speak to me like that? Who do you think you are?"

But instead, she owned it. She admitted that everything Jesus said was true. A deep level of courage is required to be authentic. And honesty with yourself and honesty with God are two of the most courageous choices you can make.

Here is what I want you to see in this encounter. First, Jesus wasn't offended by her brokenness or past; He invited it into the conversation. Second, Jesus had to go through Samaria, not to meet with a well-put-together religious leader, not to have lunch with a high-net-worth business guy who could fund His ministry, and not to set an appointment with a renowned politician who could broker peace between the Jews and the Samaritans.

Jesus had to go through Samaria to talk with a Samaritan woman who didn't know who He was; she wasn't a follower of Jesus. She had been broken and used, left, and abandoned. Her reputation had her going to the well during the hottest part of the day so she could avoid uncomfortable conversations.

Yet she responded with humility (I need something only You can give, Jesus) and courage (You are right about me, Jesus). She wasn't offended by Jesus calling out her past or promiscuity; she felt freed by it.

commitment

Courage takes place in the moment, but we need an ongoing commitment to authenticity. The final piece of the DNA of authenticity takes place over time. It's that commitment that has the greatest impact—on us and on those around us.

> Then, leaving her water jar, the woman went back to the town and said to the people, "Come, see a man who told me everything I ever did. Could this be the Messiah?" They came out of the town and made their way toward him. (John 4:28–30)

Your commitment to an authentic life always involves others. This is my interpretation, but the woman leaving her water jar at the well feels symbolic. She had carried this empty jar and empty love life to the well, hoping to get water, and had encountered the living water of Jesus. Jesus had exposed all the wounded, broken, dysfunctional parts of her heart, called out her sin, and told her He was the Messiah. She had acknowledged her sin, humbled herself, asked for help, dared to be honest, and left the old life she brought at the feet of Jesus.

Her first response was to return to her town and tell the people that Jesus had just called out her sin. Meaning, she returned to the people she was trying to avoid by going to the well at noon in the heat of the day. She faced them and told them that He could be the Messiah.

> Your commitment to an authentic life always involves others.

More people are attending church today than at any other time in history. Many people are going to church, but very few are changing. For a lot of us, the Church isn't a place for healing, but rather a place to conceal our wounds. We come to church like the woman went to the well. We are hoping to avoid people, issues, and truth. We've learned that pretending is more acceptable than being authentic.

Authenticity is the cry of many but the game of few.

I don't know where you are today. Maybe you have realized that you can't erase your past, so you are trying to outrun it and are tired and worn out. Self-awareness could be your first step to healing. Maybe your life is filled with fear and regret, and you've confused shame with humility. This is a great time to come to Jesus and admit you need something only He can give. Maybe you have tried so hard to hide your wounds or mistakes, and defensiveness is the posture of your heart. It takes courage to be authentic. Perhaps you have people in your life whose lives would be transformed if you allowed God to change your heart. It will take commitment, but it will be worth it.

I can tell you from personal experience that the pathway to transformation is authenticity. God can't change the parts of our hearts we refuse to give to Him. It's messy, but it's beautiful. Transformation comes as we are honest with God, ourselves, and others. God doesn't transform perfect people; He transforms authentic people.

chapter 3

come out of hiding

when fear sends us into hiding, authenticity is the casualty

> *"Concealment makes the soul a swamp; confession is how you drain it."*
>
> Charles M. Blow, *Fire Shut Up in My Bones*

When our oldest son, Micah, was in second grade, I got an unexpected call from his teacher. I was in a meeting at the time, so she left a voice mail asking if my wife or I could meet with her as soon as possible. Trisha was out of town, so I called her to see if she'd already talked with the teacher and if she knew what the meeting request was about. My wife, bless her heart, rarely knows where her phone is, so the probability of her talking to the teacher before me was slim to none. Nevertheless, I knew I would earn good husband points by asking. So, I'll remove any suspense you may be feeling—she hadn't talked to the teacher or even checked her voice mail.

Trish and I theorized about what the subject of the meeting could be. Micah is brilliant and driven; maybe he took a test, they realized how extraordinary he is, and they wanted to move him to a special class for gifted kids? It was early in the school year, but maybe she had already recognized Micah's leadership ability and wanted to talk to us about how to leverage his influence for positive good in her classroom? The possibilities were endless. And with Micah, calls like this were always good news.

I called the teacher back and introduced myself. She immediately said, "Are you available to meet today after school?" Her voice didn't carry an "I have amazing news to share with you about your overachieving, brilliant son" tone. Instead, she sounded concerned. I said, "Does this need to be in person, or can we talk about it over the phone?" She said, "I have some concerns about Micah that I need to discuss in person."

I was stunned. I sat there for a few seconds, not knowing how to respond. Finally, I said, "Are you sure you have the right son? Micah is my oldest and a rule follower who never gets in trouble. You might have him confused with his younger brother Elijah. We get calls like this all the time about Elijah." She said, "No, this is about Micah. Are you able to come in today?"

I'm not trying to judge this teacher's heart, but when I arrived, it felt like she was playing a power trip on me. She sat behind her desk and asked me to sit in one of the desks—a second-grade desk. I'm 6'3"; this was a very tight squeeze.

I sat down and asked what was going on. She said, "I like having Micah in class, but we have an issue I need to discuss."

I said, "Okay."

"Micah failed a test."

I thought, *Is this the meeting-in-person-worthy offense you needed to talk to me about immediately?* I said, "Failing a test is somewhat unusual for Micah." Actually, he'd never failed a test in his life, but I didn't want to be smug. "Is that what you needed to talk to me about? I didn't know Micah failed the test."

She said, "I know you didn't know. I asked Micah to bring his test home a few days ago to have you sign it and offered him a retake."

I said, "Well, I never saw the test."

She said, "I know; the test is over there. I just found it today." She pointed over to a trash can in the corner of the room. I looked at her. She looked at me. An awkward silence passed until I realized she wanted me to go get it.

So, I pried myself out of the desk and walked over to the trash can. Pulling out the wadded-up paper, I saw on top of the spelling test Micah's name and a big red "F-SEE ME" with a circle around it.

I thought, *That's a little overkill. What second-grade teacher writes an F that large on my advanced and accelerated kid's paper? The audacity.*

She said, "I was happy to give Micah a second chance; all he had to do was share the grade with you."

Micah was sitting out in the hallway, and she asked him to come in. When he walked into the room and saw the failed test in my hand, tears welled up in his eyes. I said, "Buddy, what happened with your test?"

"I failed it. I'm a failure. I failed it."

I said, "I know you failed it. It's okay that you failed it. It's one test. Why did you throw it away? You could have had another chance. You could have had a retake."

He said, "I knew that I failed. I didn't want you to know I failed. I want you to be proud of me. I thought if I hid it from you, you wouldn't know."

I said, "Micah, my love for you isn't based on your test scores. My love for you isn't based on your performance. I love you, and I'm proud of you."

Now, to honor the deal I made to get his permission to share this story with you, Micah asked me to let you know he did study for that test. He was prepared for the test. According to him, though, I had him study the wrong week's spelling words. That's not how I remember it.

We are born with a predisposition to hide. No one teaches us to conceal. No one teaches us to skirt the truth. It's almost a reflex. It's almost natural.

Our instinct to hide doesn't only go back to the time when we were young; it goes back to the very first human beings, Adam and Eve.

fully known, fully loved

Genesis 1–2 says God created the heavens and the earth. Then, He looked at all He had made and said, "It is good." Later, on the sixth day, He created Adam. But God said, "It is not good for the man to be alone" (Gen. 2:18), so He created woman.

Adam and Eve had a unique relationship with God. They were fully exposed before God, and they felt entirely comfortable. They were naked and not ashamed. They were fully known, and they felt fully loved. Imagine a relationship in which there is no shame. No compulsion to cover up. No desire to hide. You are fully exposed, and you feel fully loved.

God's desire for you is that you would be fully known and know that you are fully loved.

God created this incredible home for Adam and Eve, He provided them with all they could ever need, and He gave them purpose and meaning and His presence. Then He said they could have anything they wanted in the garden except for one thing: the tree located in the middle of the garden. He told them to stay away from it or they would die. It wasn't good for them.

our tendency to hide

But then, in Genesis 3, the serpent appeared and twisted God's words to get Eve to question God's goodness. She started to believe that God was holding out on her and keeping her from all the fun.

> The woman was convinced. She saw that the tree was
> beautiful and its fruit looked delicious, and she wanted

the wisdom it would give her. So she took some of the fruit and ate it. Then she gave some to her husband, who was with her, and he ate it, too. At that moment their eyes were opened, and they suddenly felt shame at their nakedness. So they sewed fig leaves together to cover themselves.

When the cool evening breezes were blowing, the man and his wife heard the LORD God walking about in the garden. So they hid from the LORD God among the trees. Then the LORD God called to the man, "Where are you?"

He replied, "I heard you walking in the garden, so I hid. I was afraid because I was naked."

"Who told you that you were naked?" the LORD God asked. "Have you eaten from the tree whose fruit I commanded you not to eat?"

The man replied, "It was the woman you gave me who gave me the fruit, and I ate it."

Then the LORD God asked the woman, "What have you done?"

"The serpent deceived me," she replied. "That's why I ate it." (Gen. 3:6–13 NLT)

Why did Adam hide? In his own words, "I heard you walking in the garden, so I hid. I was afraid because I was naked."

Fear, sin, and hiding go hand in hand. There is a cause and effect when we allow fear to direct our lives. Sin causes distance in relationships. Hiding keeps distance in relationships. Sin causes pain in relationships. Hiding keeps a relationship broken. Sin causes a disconnection with God. Hiding keeps us disconnected from God. Sin affects those in our immediate circle. Hiding can affect generations.

the example of David

In King David's life, we've seen a man anointed to do great things for God. He was set apart to be the king of Israel and a spiritual leader of God's people. He knew God's heart, and God knew his. From the time David slayed a giant as a boy to the time of his becoming king over all of Israel, God was with him.

One afternoon, David was on the roof of his palace, and he saw a woman bathing. Captivated by her beauty, he sent one of his messengers to find out more about this woman. His messenger returned to explain that she was the wife of Uriah, a faithful soldier in the Israelite army, who was away at war, fighting for David.

At this moment, David knew exactly who Bathsheba was. In 1 Chronicles 11, Uriah the Hittite was listed as one of David's mighty warriors. He was one of about forty men who had fought with and for David in the most epic of battles. Uriah was very close—in proximity, if not regular camaraderie—to David.

But even knowing this, David overlooked what Uriah had done for him and made a terrible decision. It is a story you are probably familiar with: David sent for Bathsheba and slept with her. *No one will know*, he thought. He was the king and had the power to keep things quiet. But sin has a way of revealing itself, even when we think we can hide it. A short time later, Bathsheba realized she was pregnant.

> Sin causes a disconnection
> with God. Hiding keeps us
> disconnected from God.

Faced with his actions, David continued lying, rather than telling the truth. He called Uriah back from battle, invited him to the palace, and then sent him home to sleep with his wife, so David could cover up the pregnancy. But Uriah was so loyal to the king that he refused to go home. The next day, David invited Uriah back to the palace to convince him to go home and sleep with his wife, even getting him drunk. But again, Uriah refused, out of loyalty to David and his fellow soldiers. Finally, David was forced to escalate his cover-up scheme; he had Uriah put on the front lines of the battle, so that he would be killed (2 Sam. 11).

When David committed adultery, he covered up what he had done from those around him, but even worse, he hid from God. Like Adam and Eve in the garden, David attempted to deal with sin by hiding it.

the example of Janiyah

In 2016, Trisha and I were in the early stage of starting Hope City Church, developing a launch team, and doing preview worship services and special events. We encouraged our small launch team to invite their friends to our next cookout, worship service, or service project each week. Our son Isaiah was in sixth grade at the time and handed out invites to his football team. One of Isaiah's teammates, Otto Kyler, along with his mom (Tina) and dad (Steve), showed up at our next worship service. It was a cool moment that was only exceeded when Otto raised his hand a few weeks later to accept

Christ. He was the first person baptized at Hope City Church. From that moment, our family and the Kylers have shared a special connection.

A year later, our son Elijah was just days away from graduating high school, and we were scrambling to buy everyone graduation outfits. We took an urgent trip to the mall to ensure everyone was set for the big day. As we were walking through Macy's, I got a text message from Tina. Tina owned an adoption agency and regularly told us about the infants she helped find new homes through the beauty of adoption. Her text said, "Hey Justin, I just emailed you and Trisha a PDF profile. I think you should pray about it and get back to me."

I paused in the middle of the store and pulled up the email. Trish stopped and asked what was wrong. I said, "Tina just texted and asked that we pray about something. I'm trying to figure out what she wants us to pray about." When I opened my email, I saw a PDF profile of two kids: Jailyn, age nine, and Janiyah, age seven. They were the oldest of five kids from Indianapolis. Tina's email said, "God laid you guys on my heart for these kids. Would you pray about this?"

Trish looked at me and said, "Wow. What do you think we should do?"

"Does she want us to adopt them, or does she want us to help her find them a home?" I asked.

"She wants us to pray about adopting them," Trish said.

Our oldest son was in college. Our second-born son, Elijah, was three days away from graduating. We were two-thirds of the way to having every-one out of the house. Now someone from our less-than-a-year-old church plant wanted me, a professional prayer, to pray about adopting these kids? She couldn't play the prayer card on me!

I texted her back, "Hey Tina, I got your email. To clarify, you want us to pray about adopting them? If so, what is the timeline for that?"

She texted back, "Yes. The birth mom would like to talk to you on Monday."

I texted back, "Today is Thursday. You mean four days from now????"

A one-word response followed from Tina, "Yes."

Elijah graduated on Sunday, June 4, 2017. We talked to the birth mom on Monday, June 5, 2017. We got emergency custody of Jailyn and Janiyah on Thursday, June 22, 2017. Yes, I am serious. Our adoption was finalized in November 2017, but we consider June 22 their "Gotcha Day."

Because of the speed of this process, Tina didn't have very much background information about the kids. None of us knew of all the foster homes they'd lived in. We didn't know about the abuse they'd gone through or the shelters they'd stayed in when they were evicted from their apartment. So, they began to tell us stories that would simultaneously break our hearts and infuriate us. I don't want to share the details of those stories, because they are Jailyn's and Janiyah's stories to tell. But because of all that these kids had gone through, they had developed a predisposition to lying and hiding that they both brought into our family.

With my daughter's blessing, I want to share of the first time Janiyah lied to me—something I'll never forget. The kids had been with us a few weeks, and I went upstairs to ensure they were getting ready for bed. They had been upstairs less than two minutes before my arrival. Janiyah was in bed, and I went to tuck her in. As I leaned down, her breath didn't smell like toothpaste; it smelled like what we had for dinner. I said, "You have all your stuff done?" She said, "Yes, Daddy."

As a father of three biological sons, hearing your new daughter call you "Daddy" is enough to melt your heart. I snapped out of it enough to say, "You put on lotion?"

"Yes," she said.

"You brushed your teeth?"

She smiled really big and said, "Yes, Daddy."

I leaned down and said, "Breathe on me real big." She blew her onion breath square in my face. Then, in a half-joking, half-serious way, I said, "Janiyah, you didn't brush your teeth."

"Yes, I did, Dad."

Now I changed my tone of voice so she would know I was serious, "Janiyah, I can smell your breath, and I can tell you didn't brush your teeth. You don't have to lie to me. Just get out of bed and brush your teeth."

She doubled down. "I did brush my teeth; why don't you believe me?"

"I don't believe you because you are lying. You didn't brush your teeth, and I don't appreciate you not telling me the truth."

"I am telling you the truth."

I said, "Janiyah, I am going to go in the bathroom, and I am going to feel your toothbrush, and if your toothbrush isn't wet, I will know you are lying, and you will be grounded. This is your last chance to tell me the truth."

"I brushed my teeth." She was lying through her teeth.

I went into the bathroom, and her toothbrush was as dry as any toothbrush has ever been in the history of toothbrushes. Now I was angry. I walked back into her room, stomping my feet along the way, so she knew I was coming. I said, "Janiyah, get out of that bed right now and come in the bathroom with me." She came in stone faced.

Trish was walking up the stairs as Janiyah and I entered the bathroom. I said, "Janiyah, this toothbrush is bone dry. You didn't brush your teeth. At this point, I don't care about you brushing your teeth. They are all baby teeth and are going to fall out anyway. What I care about is you lying to me."

With a demeanor that would have passed any polygraph test, she said, "Dad, the fancy toothbrush you bought me has a fast-drying feature. It must have dried on my way from the bathroom to the bed. I brushed my teeth; that toothbrush just dries really fast."

She said it so convincingly I momentarily thought her argument had validity. I said, "Janiyah, you are grounded from your Barbies all day tomorrow for lying to me." With a cry and wail that none of my biological male kids had ever uttered, Janiyah erupted into tears and ran and threw herself into bed. Trish and I walked over to her door and said, "I love you. Good night." And we shut the door.

A few minutes later, we heard banging coming from upstairs. It wasn't enough to be alarmed, but it caused us to wonder, "What are they doing up there?" The banging and slamming got more frequent and more intense. I went upstairs to see what was going on, and every Barbie toy, doll, and outfit was lying scattered in the hallway. I walked into Janiyah's room, and she wasn't in bed. I went into the bathroom, and she wasn't in there. I peeked in our bedroom, and she wasn't in there. I walked back into her room and said, "Janiyah." I could hear crying coming from the closet.

I opened the closet door, and at the back of the closet was a pile of hangup clothes that had been pulled off their hangers and were now on top of our daughter. I said, "Janiyah, what are you doing?"

"I'm hiding from you. You are mad at me, so I'm hiding from you."

the example of Moses

When we first encounter Moses as an adult, we see him burying the body of an Egyptian in the sand.

> Many years later, when Moses had grown up, he went
> out to visit his own people, the Hebrews, and he saw how

> hard they were forced to work. During his visit, he saw an
> Egyptian beating one of his fellow Hebrews. (Ex. 2:11 NLT)

If you grew up in church or watched *The Prince of Egypt,* you are familiar with the context of Moses' life. Moses was born during a time of slavery and oppression of the Israelite people. The pharaoh at the time was threatened by the Jewish people and concerned they would overtake the Egyptian people, so he ordered all male babies under two years old to be killed. In both rebellion and desperation, Moses' mom put Moses in a basket and floated him down the river. His sister followed him from a distance and saw as, thankfully, Moses was found by Pharaoh's daughter and brought into the palace.

Through the sovereignty of God, Moses' mom was brought into the palace as a slave and allowed to care for Moses. Moses was given a new name and a new identity, and was raised as an Egyptian, even though he was Jewish. He was surrounded daily by his people being oppressed and abused by the Egyptian people. Abandonment, trauma, identity, anger—all of this pain came to a head when he saw how his people were being treated.

> During his visit, he saw an Egyptian beating one of his
> fellow Hebrews. After looking in all directions to make
> sure no one was watching, Moses killed the Egyptian and
> hid the body in the sand.
>
> The next day, when Moses went out to visit his
> people again, he saw two Hebrew men fighting. "Why are
> you beating up your friend?" Moses said to the one who
> had started the fight.

The man replied, "Who appointed you to be our prince and judge? Are you going to kill me as you killed that Egyptian yesterday?"

Then Moses was afraid, thinking, "Everyone knows what I did." And sure enough, Pharaoh heard what had happened, and he tried to kill Moses. But Moses fled from Pharaoh and went to live in the land of Midian.

When Moses arrived in Midian, he sat down beside a well. Now the priest of Midian had seven daughters who came as usual to draw water and fill the water troughs for their father's flocks. But some other shepherds came and chased them away. So Moses jumped up and rescued the girls from the shepherds. Then he drew water for their flocks.

When the girls returned to Reuel, their father, he asked, "Why are you back so soon today?"

"An Egyptian rescued us from the shepherds," they answered. "And then he drew water for us and watered our flocks."

"Then where is he?" their father asked. "Why did you leave him there? Invite him to come and eat with us."

Moses accepted the invitation, and he settled there with him. In time, Reuel gave Moses his daughter Zipporah to be his wife. (Ex. 2:11–21 NLT)

how we hide from sin

There are many ways we try to manage our sins. The first way in which Moses responded to his sin was to bury it. "After looking in all directions to make sure no one was watching, Moses killed the Egyptian and hid the body in the sand."

Some of our deepest regrets are born when we think no one is watching. Moses looked in both directions to make sure no one was watching. Think about all he leveraged at that moment. He was an orphan. God rescued him by allowing his life to be spared when he was a baby. Not only was his life spared, but he was also found by Pharaoh's daughter and raised as royalty in the house of Pharaoh. After looking in all directions, he cashed in all of God's provisions, plans, and blessings and murdered an Egyptian. Then, he buried the body in the sand.

If you are honest, you sometimes try to deal with the sin in your life by burying it. If you can ignore the sin, then maybe it will go away. To be clear, when we talk about our sins, I'm not just talking about the sinful choices you've made and tried to bury. I'm also talking about the sinful choices that others have made against you. Some of the sins you deal with aren't choices you've made; they are choices someone else made that have affected your life.

> Sin affects those in our immediate circle. Hiding can affect generations.

You buried the abuse you experienced as a kid. You buried the abandonment you felt when your dad left. You buried the heartache you experienced when your mom passed away. You buried the rejection of getting fired. You buried the pain of your divorce. You thought you could avoid the pain by burying the past, but that's not how healing works.

After Moses buried the body, he ran away. "But Moses fled from Pharaoh and went to live in the land of Midian."

Maybe that is your story. You run from your sin. You run from your mistakes. You run from your regrets. When one relationship fails, you run to the next one. When one friendship dissolves, you run to the next one. When one job isn't what you think it should be, you run to the next one. When one marriage isn't what you think you deserve, you run to the next one.

Two things happen when you try to outrun sin and regret. First, you end up exhausted. Nothing in your life is ever resolved. You are the victim, and everyone else is wrong. Second, it always catches up to you. You know your sin has caught up to you when you start repeating it.

One of the most significant, defining moments of my life came in the counseling session after I confessed to Trish and our counselor the sexual abuse I had experienced and my pornography addiction. Our counselor said, "Unconfessed sin always leads to repeated behavior." It was a statement that defined my entire life. I had tried to bury my sin and outrun it, and it always caught up to me.

What happened next with Moses? He just settled there. "Moses accepted the invitation, and he settled there with him." Moses left Egypt and ran to Midian. For the next forty years, he was cut off from everything he'd ever known. He hid as a fugitive in Midian.

where we hide from sin

When confronted with the reality of our sin, we all have a hiding place. Micah hid his paper in the trash can. Adam and Eve hid behind fig leaves. David hid in the palace while his mighty men were on the battlefield. Janiyah hid in the closet. Moses hid in Midian.

It's easy to look at the account of Adam and Eve and think, *How ridiculous to think you could fool God by hiding behind fig leaves.*

How foolish was David to try to hide a pregnancy by bringing Uriah home from battle?

How naive of Janiyah to think she could disappear under a pile of clothes in the back of the closet.

You have a hiding place. You have a place you to go to escape your sin. You have a place you go to when running from your regrets. We all have a hiding place. Here is how I define a hiding place:

I turn to _____ to escape a choice, consequence, or outcome.

Some of our hiding places are more socially acceptable than others. Pastor Steve Carter, in his book *The Thing Beneath the Thing*, said:

> Consider for a moment how you interact with any of these seemingly innocuous things within a typical month in your life:
>
> - Television
> - Your job
> - Social media
> - Travel
> - Online shopping
> - Your children
> - Studying
> - Serving
> - Friendships
> - Food
> - Sex[1]

To come out of hiding, we must first identify where we hide. Maybe you are hiding in your busyness or schedule. Perhaps you are hiding in alcohol, drugs, Netflix, pornography, or your job. Where are you turning to escape a choice, consequence, or outcome?

why we hide from sin

The final requirement to coming out of hiding is identifying why we hide. If we don't know where we hide, we'll continue to use good things in our lives for unhealthy purposes. If we don't know why we hide, we'll continue to allow fear to send us into hiding, and authenticity will be the casualty.

We've already identified the primary motivation for hiding is fear, but three specific fears trigger our compulsion to hide.

fear of being found out

When we hide, we don't experience intimacy in the way God intended. The word *intimacy* means "to be fully known." It's the picture of God walking with Adam and Eve in the cool of the day. It's the image of them being naked but not feeling shame. That is intimacy.

When we hide from God, or we hide from the people we love, we place a cap on the amount of intimacy we're capable of experiencing. When we fear being found out, we withhold ourselves from those we care about most. That fear overtakes our hearts, and we feel stress. We imagine worst-case scenarios and allow the fear of being found out to do more damage to relationships than simply being honest would do. Most of the time, trying to hide the truth only leads us to what we fear the most: being found out. See the story of David.

fear of not being loved

Our greatest desire is intimacy—to be known. Our greatest fear is that God and others won't love us. So often, we compromise being known on the altar of being loved. We can only be loved to the extent that we are known. So, every time we sacrifice honesty and authenticity for acceptance and love, we limit our capacity to be truly loved. We know in our hearts that God or another person isn't loving the real us.

fear of emotional pain

We don't want to be exposed because we've calculated the emotional pain our secrets, lies, addictions, or confessions will cause, and we have concluded that the emotional pain we would endure or the emotional pain we would cause would be greater than any good that could come from being exposed. So, we continue to hide. We pretend that things are better than they are, thinking we are sparing ourselves and those we love from emotional pain. We are convinced that if we were exposed, and if our secret were found out, the emotional distress it would cause would make us unlovable.

A few months ago, I was counseling a guy and weighing the cost of telling his wife about his porn addiction. They were having marriage problems, and he wanted help. We discovered his disposition of defensiveness when it came to his wife. Even when she wasn't accusing him of anything, he met her requests or suggestions with immediate defensiveness.

I said, "Don't you think the root of your defensiveness is the hiddenness you're living with right now? You have this guilt for the sin in your heart, and it's coming out as defensiveness." He agreed that was the motivation, so I encouraged him to confess his porn addiction to his wife.

His response could be all our reactions when considering coming out of hiding. He said, "If I tell her that I'm addicted to pornography, it will hurt her. I don't want to hurt her."

I said, "You are hurting your wife; she just doesn't know. You don't think you are hurting her by hiding this, but the pain you're causing now is destructive pain. Confession will be painful, but it will be a redemptive pain."

Let's go back to the story of David. He had already committed adultery and murder. The king of Israel—in no uncertain terms—had sinned. Not only had he sinned, but he had also hidden his sin from God. For almost an entire year, this sin went unconfessed. Finally, God had enough, and He confronted David.

In 2 Samuel 12, we read that God sent the prophet Nathan to confront David's sin, to lower the waterline of his heart and expose the iceberg he'd been hiding:

> So the LORD sent Nathan the prophet to tell David this story: "There were two men in a certain town. One was rich, and one was poor. The rich man owned a great many sheep and cattle. The poor man owned nothing but one little lamb he had bought. He raised that little lamb, and it grew up with his children. It ate from the man's own plate and drank from his cup. He cuddled it in his arms like a baby daughter. One day a guest arrived at the home of the rich man. But instead of killing an animal from his own flock or herd, he took the poor man's lamb and killed it and prepared it for his guest."

David was furious. "As surely as the LORD lives," he vowed, "any man who would do such a thing deserves to die! He must repay four lambs to the poor man for the one he stole and for having no pity."

Then Nathan said to David, "You are that man!"

(2 Sam. 12:1–7 NLT)

This is what I love about the story of David: with those four words—You are that man!—his entire life was exposed. Most of the time, like David, we too wait until we are told before we realize the tremendous freedom in coming out of hiding. David was exposed, and in the process of being exposed, he discovered the power of confession.

Look what David said in Psalm 32:1–7:

Blessed is the one
    whose transgressions are forgiven,
    whose sins are covered.
Blessed is the one
    whose sin the LORD does not count against them
    and in whose spirit is no deceit.

When I kept silent,
    my bones wasted away
    through my groaning all day long.
For day and night
    your hand was heavy on me;
my strength was sapped
    as in the heat of summer.

> Then I acknowledged my sin to you
>   and did not cover up my iniquity.
> I said, "I will confess
>   my transgressions to the LORD."
> And you forgave
>   the guilt of my sin.
>
> Therefore let all the faithful pray to you
>   while you may be found;
> surely the rising of the mighty waters
>   will not reach them.
> You are my hiding place;
>   you will protect me from trouble
>   and surround me with songs of deliverance.

Maybe you are in a similar place. You are wasting away because you are silent about your sin. You have secrets, mistakes, and things you have convinced yourself that you can never confess. You are tired.

Did you catch what David said in verse 7 of Psalm 32? "You are my hiding place."

Life is lived differently when you stop trying to hide your sins and allow God Himself to be your hiding place. When God is your hiding place, you don't have to hide. When God is your hiding place, you don't have to try to be loved; you know you are loved. When God is your hiding place, you don't have to pretend. When God is your hiding place, you place yourself on the path from inauthentic to real.

part two

the path from
perfect to real

chapter 4

realize brokenness is not weakness

our greatest transformation comes as
we become desperate for Jesus

> *"A saint is not someone who is good but who experiences the goodness*
> *of God."*
>
> Thomas Merton

Our family relocated to Nashville, Tennessee, in July 2009, to go on staff at Cross Point Church. As a lifelong Indianapolis Colts fan, I entered AFC South enemy territory by moving to the home of the Tennessee Titans. But even Titan fans need Jesus.

In September, the Titans started the 2009 season playing against the Pittsburgh Steelers on a Thursday night. It was a big game, and some friends from church invited our family over for a kickoff party and dinner. My son Elijah was in fifth grade and had flag-football practice that night. Trisha had a meeting at church and was going to arrive at the party after kickoff.

It was up to me to pick up the kids from school, get Elijah to flag-football practice, and then make it to the party before kickoff. There is no easy way to drive anywhere in Nashville, with its hills and traffic and winding roads. If

everything went well, it would still be a challenge to get from football practice to the football party before kickoff.

Elijah was the first of our kids to play flag football. The year prior, he'd
played tackle football in Indiana, but Nashville didn't offer tackle football
for his age-group. Flag-football practice involved a lot of drills, and a lot of
passing and catching, but no contact.

I was watching the practice while sitting in the van with the other two
boys to communicate to Elijah that I wanted to leave quickly after he was
done. On the last play of the final drill, Elijah went out for a pass, caught
the ball, and fell awkwardly to the ground. He started holding his wrist and
crying a little. The coaches walked out onto the field and knelt next to Elijah
to check on him. One of them stood up and motioned for me to come to the
field. I looked at the clock in the van, then got out of the car.

When I got to Elijah, I asked him if he was okay. He said, "No, I think I
broke my arm."

I said, "Buddy, that's impossible. You are playing flag football. There is
no contact. You didn't break your arm. You probably sprained it. Let's get in
the car; we'll put some ice on it at the party."

We got in the car and sped across Nashville in the direction of the party.
On our way, Micah gave his prognosis: "Dad, I think Elijah broke his arm. It's
really swollen."

"We'll put some ice on it when we get to the party. I really don't think
it's broken," I said.

We arrived at the party, and Elijah walked in holding his arm like it was
dislocated from the shoulder, elbow, and wrist. About twenty other people
were there, and half of those in attendance were mothers. One hundred percent of the moms informed me that we should leave the party and go to the
emergency room.

Emergency room? That would be expensive and take forever. It was flag football. Elijah was a tough kid. His arm wasn't broken. I got him some ice, sat him down in a comfortable chair with large armrests, put his arm on an armrest and the ice on his arm, and began to watch the game.

Every few minutes, another person walked over to Elijah, lifted up the ice, examined his arm, and then looked at me with judgment and condemnation. Elijah kept looking up, with his soft brown eyes, and saying in a raspy voice, "My dad doesn't think it's broken."

Just before halftime, my wife arrived at the party. I have to admit that Elijah's arm was pretty swollen by then. As Trish walked in the front door, it felt like every ounce of air was sucked out of the room. Everyone got quiet and stopped moving. I think someone hit "mute" on the TV.

At this point, I'd been married fourteen years and was wise enough to text my wife and let her know Elijah was hurt. I told her it wasn't that big of a deal and that we'd put ice on it. When she entered the room, every female available formed a V-formation around her, and they all walked over to surround Elijah.

Trish lifted the ice pack from Elijah's arm. The look she gave me is seared into my memory. "Get your stuff; we're going to the hospital," she said.

Bottom line—his arm was broken. In two places. From playing flag football.

This isn't a story about how incompetent a father I am; although, it may provide some kind of evidence.

This is my life. This is your life. We are broken and hurt, wounded and fractured. We put ice on it. We compartmentalize our lives, or we numb the pain. There is a party going on, and everyone knows we're broken, but we are content with the ice pack.

the "broken" at the Pharisee's party

In Luke 7, Jesus was invited to a party, but it wasn't an NFL kickoff party. This was a dinner party at the home of a Pharisee. There were at least two broken people at this party; one already knew it and one was about to find out.

When one of the Pharisees invited Jesus to have dinner with him, he went to the Pharisee's house and reclined at the table. A woman in that town who lived a sinful life learned that Jesus was eating at the Pharisee's house, so she came there with an alabaster jar of perfume. As she stood behind him at his feet weeping, she began to wet his feet with her tears. Then she wiped them with her hair, kissed them and poured perfume on them.

When the Pharisee who had invited him saw this, he said to himself, "If this man were a prophet, he would know who is touching him and what kind of woman she is—that she is a sinner."

Jesus answered him, "Simon, I have something to tell you."

"Tell me, teacher," he said.

"Two people owed money to a certain moneylender. One owed him five hundred denarii, and the other fifty. Neither of them had the money to pay him back, so he forgave the debts of both. Now which of them will love him more?"

Simon replied, "I suppose the one who had the bigger debt forgiven."

"You have judged correctly," Jesus said.

Then he turned toward the woman and said to Simon, "Do you see this woman? I came into your house. You did not give me any water for my feet, but she wet my feet with her tears and wiped them with her hair. You did not give me a kiss, but this woman, from the time I entered, has not stopped kissing my feet. You did not put oil on my head, but she has poured perfume on my feet. Therefore, I tell you, her many sins have been forgiven—as her great love has shown. But whoever has been forgiven little loves little."

Then Jesus said to her, "Your sins are forgiven."

The other guests began to say among themselves, "Who is this who even forgives sins?"

Jesus said to the woman, "Your faith has saved you; go in peace." (Luke 7:36–50)

My wife has the gift of hospitality. I do not. She has a keen sense of what should be done in our house to prepare for a guest. There are dishes to be done, toilets to clean, laundry to put away, and clean sheets to put on the beds. There is vacuuming, sweeping, and dusting. Certain things happen at our house every time we host a guest.

As a rabbi, Jesus was likely the guest of honor at the Pharisee's dinner. Preparations had been made, but also certain customs had to be observed for a guest as honored as Jesus.

the host's responsibilities

The first responsibility was a customary greeting. The host greeted the guest with a kiss upon their arrival. If the guest were a person of equal status, the kiss was on the cheek; but if it were a person of higher importance or stature than the host, the kiss was on the guest's hand. To not do this was insulting at worst and indifferent at best. It was the equivalent of ignoring your guest when they came over or not shaking their hand.

Another custom involved the washing of feet. This was mandatory for meals. We tell our kids to wash their hands before dinner; the people in biblical times would always wash their feet. They wore sandals, and they walked everywhere. The roads were dusty, and their feet got funky. If the guest were of high status, the host would wash their feet themselves. If they weren't of a high class, then the host's servant would be responsible for washing the guest's feet upon arrival. At minimum, the host provided the guest water to wash their own feet.

Sometimes, if the journey was long or the guest was highly esteemed, the host would anoint the head of the guest with olive oil. The anointing of oil was a sign of refreshment. The oil wouldn't necessarily be expensive, but it would be a nice gesture.

At this dinner, Jesus was a visiting rabbi who had been teaching all day. When He arrived, nothing happened. There was no kiss of greeting, no washing of feet, and no anointing with oil. These weren't subtle miscues. They indicated that Jesus was ignored. We can assume that Simon intended to make a silent statement to Jesus and everyone in attendance—to show Jesus up publicly.

the woman's generosity

Then, another guest arrived at the dinner; she was uninvited. The Holman New Testament Commentary helps us make sense of what happened: "The meal was apparently a special, public celebration, possibly connected with the Sabbath or another Jewish festival. At such times outsiders could enter the open door, sit by the wall, watch, and perhaps beg for leftover scraps."[1]

Dinners like this took place in the outer courtyard of the host's home. In our day, it would be like having a party in our front yard, or perhaps on our deck. Only the invited guests could eat, but anyone who wanted could come to the party and observe. All that sets up verse 37: The woman, who had "lived a sinful life" showed up at Jesus' feet. The English Standard Version says, "And behold, a woman of the city, who was a sinner." The Tyndale New Testament Commentary says, *"A woman of the city* described as *a sinner,* which probably means a prostitute."[2]

The phrases "sinful life" and "woman of the city" both meant that the woman was considered a prostitute. She was not just a sinful woman; she was a professionally sinful woman. People at the dinner party likely knew who she was; the text says that Simon, at least, knew about her. Her reputation preceded her.

Luke didn't record the woman's name. We don't know much about her other than her reputation and that she owned at least one alabaster jar of perfume. Maybe the perfume was a tool of her profession. One thing I think we can assume is that she didn't set out to become a prostitute. She didn't wake up when she was a little girl dreaming of the day she would sell her body, and be used and abused. Instead, I imagine that, every day of her adult life, she wondered, *How did I end up here? How did I drift so far from the dreams I once had?*

Have you ever been there? *How did I drift so far into debt? How did I drift so far away from truth-telling? How did I end up being so angry? How did I end up with so many broken relationships? How did I end up addicted to porn, alcohol, or gambling? How did I end up here?*

I've been in that place a few times in my life. One specific time was in 2011. Trish and I had done the hard work of healing our marriage. I'd spent four years out of ministry and had gone through the restoration process required before returning to pastoring. It was two years after we moved to

Nashville and I went on staff at Cross Point Church. My salary was half what I had made the previous year, and we didn't adjust our spending.

On top of that, we couldn't sell our house in Indiana before we moved. After a few months of paying rent in Nashville and mortgage in Indiana, we found tenants for the home in Indiana. What they paid us at least covered our mortgage—when they paid the rent. Unfortunately, they rarely paid rent on time and sometimes not at all.

By the end of our second year in Nashville, we had accumulated $46,000 of consumer credit-card and medical debt. We woke up to the reality of our situation when a sheriff served my wife papers. Citi Cards had filed a suit for the lack of payment on an $8,000 balance for a credit card in her name. Until then, I had been responsible for our finances, but it became apparent I wasn't financially trustworthy. The Sunday after Trish was served papers, I stood onstage at church and invited the congregation to sign up for Financial Peace University. I told them how bad debt was to their financial peace and how this class could help them be good stewards of what God had given them.

As I walked off the stage, I felt the Holy Spirit prompt me, "Did you listen to anything you just said? This class is for you." I brushed it off and went to the lobby to greet people as they left the church.

When I got home from church, Trish told me she had registered us for Financial Peace. I was not happy. I was embarrassed and ashamed. I said, "Do you know how embarrassing it will be to show up at this class, not to teach it, but to admit we have $46,000 of debt? These are people I'm supposed to be leading spiritually?"

She said, "Is it more embarrassing than having a sheriff serve you papers that a bank is suing you for non-payment? You can't lead spiritually in this area if you ignore it. We can't get out of debt until we come to terms with the depth of our debt."

I knew she was right, though it didn't make it easier. By God's grace, we went to Financial Peace and came to terms with our debt. Within eight months, we paid off every dime of that $46,000.

The woman at the Pharisee's party brought with her a large balance of debt—in sin and regret. I assume she noticed that Simon didn't perform the customary acts of greeting. We don't know what prompted her, but she moved from the sidelines of this dinner to the feet of Jesus at the table.

Our dinner customs and patterns are drastically different from those in Jesus' day. The woman moving to the feet of Jesus in our culture would involve climbing under a table and navigating the feet and legs of everyone at the table. In ancient Middle Eastern culture, the table was low to the ground, and people sat on mats or pillows around the outside of the table. The men at the dinner, including Jesus, reclined at the table on their left elbows, with their feet stretched out behind them. As Jesus reclined this way, the woman saw an opportunity to demonstrate her devotion to Him.

She didn't come to the party to try to fit in or pretend to be better than she was. Aware of her lifestyle, she didn't try to find a seat at the table; she desperately went to the feet of Jesus.

The woman approached Jesus' feet with tears streaming down her face and a perfume bottle in her hands. She lowered and used her hair to wipe the feet of Jesus with her tears and perfume. Simon had seen enough. He couldn't believe Jesus allowed her to touch Him. He was so appalled that he didn't address the woman's spiritual life directly; instead, he questioned Jesus' credentials as a spiritual authority.

> When the Pharisee who had invited him saw this, he said
> to himself, "If this man were a prophet, he would know

who is touching him and what kind of woman she is—
that she is a sinner." (Luke 7:39)

the parable Jesus told

Jesus knew all about this woman, and He knew all about Simon. So He told
this short parable.

> Two people owed money to a certain moneylender.
> One owed him five hundred denarii, and the other fifty.
> Neither of them had the money to pay him back, so he
> forgave the debts of both. Now which of them will love
> him more? (Luke 7:41–42)

Both men had debt, and neither of them could pay it back. One debt
looked manageable; the other insurmountable. Neither could pay, and so
rather than serving papers through the sheriff, the lender canceled both
debts.

After telling the story, Jesus asked Simon a self-evident question:
"Which would be more thankful?"

Simon said, "I suppose the one who had the bigger debt forgiven."

Jesus said, "You have judged correctly."

Verse 44 is the most beautiful statement in this passage: "Then he
turned toward the woman."

Picture this: Simon and everyone else at the dinner were in front of
Jesus. Jesus turned to the woman but continued His conversation with
Simon: "Do you see this woman?" The implication was, I know you've been
looking at her, Simon. You've been judging her; you've seen her occupation
and social standing, but do you *see* her?

They all looked at Jesus, and Jesus kept looking at the sinful woman, while talking to Simon: "I came to your house; you had no water for My feet. So, this woman washed My feet with her hair. I came into your home, and you offered Me no kiss; meanwhile, she has not stopped kissing My feet. I came to your house, and you provided no oil for My head. Instead, she has lavished Me with the most valuable thing she owns. She has poured her life out at My feet, Simon" (my paraphrase).

Jesus continued: "Therefore, Simon, her sins, which I know are many, are all forgiven. That's why she loves so lavishly; that's why she pours herself out at My feet; that's why her tears fall freely, and she can't stop kissing Me. Because he (or she) who has been forgiven much loves much. But the one who's forgiven little only loves little" (again, my paraphrase).

Jesus wasn't saying that Simon had only sinned a little. He didn't say that Simon was so righteous that he only needed a little grace, or that God was getting a pretty good deal with Simon. That's not what Jesus was saying.

What was He saying? It is hard to be overwhelmed by grace when you've convinced yourself you don't need it. Simon thought of himself as a small debtor and, therefore, couldn't be in awe of God's grace.

John Ortberg said this: "The question this story raises is who's really the big debtor? There is a great sin at this dinner, but it's not the sin Simon thinks it is: It is the sin of lips that won't kiss, knees that won't kneel; eyes that will not weep, hands that will not serve and perfume that will never leave the jar."[3]

what it means to be broken

Two people, each in the presence of Jesus, but on very different sides of the table.

Simon the Pharisee	Sinful Woman
Sanctified	Sinful
Accomplished	Desperate
Religious	Repentant
Put Together	Broken
Entitled	Generous
Revered	Disrespected
Performer	Poured Out
Fake	Honest

Religion can put you at the table with Jesus, but only brokenness will put you at His feet. Being at the feet of Jesus was a description of the sinful woman's physical location, but it was also her spiritual disposition. Being at the feet of Jesus is the location of brokenness.

As we turn the corner on our journey from perfect to real, the first milestone is to realize brokenness is not weakness. On the contrary, the spiritual condition of brokenness is a prerequisite to authenticity.

The word *brokenness* can be used in a spiritually negative way. We've used it in this book to describe fractured relationships, wounded hearts, and sinful patterns. That is unhealthy brokenness. But for the remainder of the chapter, I want to focus on an alternate use of brokenness.

> Religion can put you at the table with Jesus, but only brokenness will put you at His feet.

Dr. Eric Mason, a pastor and author, gave an insightful definition of the type of brokenness that produces the authenticity we long for. He said, "Brokenness is the spiritual state by which we are disarmed of our self-dependance and pride."[4]

Pastor Crawford Loritts described brokenness as "living in a constant state of God-neediness."[5]

David offered his own definition of brokenness in a passage you may be familiar with: "The LORD is close to the brokenhearted and saves those who are crushed in spirit" (Ps. 34:18).

That phrase, "crushed in spirit," is what we are talking about when it comes to brokenness. The transliteration of the Hebrew word for "crushed" is *dăk·kā*, which has several meanings:

Shattered

Devoid of arrogance

Maimed

Contrite

Injured

Smashed

Wrecked

Fractured

Disabled

God's presence is close to the brokenhearted, and He saves those crushed in spirit. For most of my life, I looked at the word *saved* almost like *rescued*. Like, God is saving us from being crushed in spirit. But when you look at the word in Hebrew, it is the word *yš'*, which can also be translated as "accepts" or "receives." Eventually, this word evolved into the Hebrew word for "Savior."

David was saying God's presence is close to the brokenhearted, and He *accepts* those who are spiritually wrecked and shattered. This is the same word David used when he articulated his brokenness and repentance over his sin with Bathsheba: "My sacrifice, O God, is a broken spirit; a broken and contrite heart you, God, will not despise" (Ps. 51:17).

The New Living Translation of that verse reinforces this: "The sacrifice you desire is a broken (*dăk·kā*) spirit. You will not reject a broken (*dăk·kā*) and repentant heart, O God."

David wasn't using the word *broken* to mean "sad" or "hurt." Notice that in the NLT translation, the words "not despise" from the NIV are translated "not reject." That translation carries forward the thought that being crushed spiritually is the prerequisite to being accepted and received by God. David realized in his own life that God accepts, saves, and doesn't despise those who are spiritually shattered, wrecked, or broken.

Brokenness is a posture of surrender; it's giving up rather than trying harder. Brokenness is a decision, laying everything on the line and then submitting it all to God. It is an awareness that God is your only hope. You can choose brokenness. God longs to see us desire brokenness, for this is where His strength is made perfect.

the "losses" of brokenness

We tend not to think about brokenness in a positive light. In our culture, it's easy to look at the cost of brokenness and ignore the benefits. But it is only in the process of surrender and loss that we gain from God what we can't attain on our own—transformation. Here are three losses that brokenness brings that become gains in our journey to being real.

your need to control

Psalm 62:8 says, "O my people, trust in him at all times. Pour out your heart to him, for God is our refuge" (NLT).

Do you see the imagery here? Pour out your heart like the sinful woman poured out her tears and perfume. Pour out your life like she poured out her worship and adoration. There is a connection to pouring out your heart and trusting Him at all times.

When you have a faulty trust in God, you don't think He can control your life as well as you can, so you manipulate. When you choose brokenness, you trust that God is in control and submit to what He desires and chooses. There's freedom in living knowing He's in control.

your need to impress

When you choose brokenness, you lose your need to impress others. You begin to live out of an identity not based on others' opinions, validations, or acceptance. When you live only trying to impress God, you discover the confidence and freedom you've been attempting to provide for yourself.

My affair in 2005 affected my wife, kids, family, and church family in devastating ways. When we started Genesis Church in 2002, God blessed us with excellent relationships with other churches and pastors in our community. Several of them gifted us money and resources. A few gave us meeting and office space until we launched public services. One of those churches was Grace Church and its pastor Dave Rodriguez. Grace was the largest church in our community and had tremendous influence. Dave treated me like his own staff member and went above and beyond to support our new church and me. He went to his board and requested that Grace gift our church $50,000 to help cover our start-up expenses. So, Dave was close to our church, and my sinful choices directly impacted him.

After a few months of separation and counseling, Trish invited me to move back home, and we planned to reconcile. Around the time I moved back home, I got a phone call from Dave. I hadn't personally talked to him since the affair was exposed. He wanted to meet with me. I had no idea what to expect at our meeting. To say I was nervous is an understatement.

> It is only in the process of surrender and loss that we gain from God what we can't attain on our own—transformation.

I arrived at Starbucks, and Dave was inside waiting for me. He stood up and hugged me, and tears filled his eyes. We sat down, and I recounted for him the long, dark journey I had made to cheat on God, my wife, the church, Dave, his staff, every person who had supported us, and so many others. I also told him of the restoration God had begun in my heart and how God had brought healing to Trisha, me, and our family through counseling. He was genuinely happy for us and proud of the steps I had taken.

At the end of our time together, he said something that changed me, my marriage, and everything I do and say to this day. He said, "I want you to know I am praying a Lamentations 3 prayer for you. Specifically, I am praying Lamentations 3:16 over you."

I had no idea what Lamentations 3 was about, nor did I know what verse 16 of Lamentations 3 said. I replied, "I really appreciate that. Do you mind telling me what Lamentations 3:16 says?"

He said, "It says that God will grab you by the back of the head and crush your teeth on gravel. That is my prayer for you."

Huh? Maybe Dave meant he was praying *John* 3:16 prayers for me. I like John 3:16. But no, he said, "If you are going to find true healing from this, God will have to destroy you first. Lamentations 3 is my prayer for you." We hugged, and I left.

When I got home that afternoon, I immediately grabbed my Bible and went to Lamentations 3:16: "He has broken my teeth with gravel; he has trampled me in the dust."

Bible scholar Martin Manser wrote this about Lamentations 3:16: "God breaks the spirit of the proud and arrogant so that in their humility and brokenness they may come to repentance and restoration."[6]

God breaks us so He can remake us. He breaks us to free us from our need to impress others and to bring us back to Him.

The sinful woman went to the feet of Jesus without regard for public opinion. She wasn't there to impress Simon. She was there to worship Jesus, to be broken before Him.

your desire to pretend

When you embrace brokenness, you stop pretending. You stop pretending you've got it all together, got all the answers, have the perfect marriage, and overcome all the sins. You lose your desire to pretend to be a better friend, husband, or parent than you are, and you desire to be more of who God calls you to be. You want to wake up and be the person you've been pretending to be, realizing that brokenness is the only way to get there. Look what Paul said in 2 Corinthians 4:7–10:

> But we have this treasure in jars of clay, to show that the
> surpassing power belongs to God and not to us. We are
> afflicted in every way, but not crushed; perplexed, but not

driven to despair; persecuted, but not forsaken; struck
down, but not destroyed; always carrying in the body
the death of Jesus, so that the life of Jesus may also be
manifested in our bodies. (ESV)

You become comfortable with your weakness when you die of your need
to impress others. You don't have to pretend to be anything but a jar of clay.
As you recognize the treasure that resides in your identity as a jar of clay,
you can then display the surpassing power that belongs to God. Brokenness
isn't weakness. Weakness is the path to the surpassing power you need for
transformation.

Most of us don't choose this path, because nothing is appealing about
it. It is what taking up your cross looks like. It means dying to yourself so
Jesus can bring you the new life He promises. It's narrow, and most of those
who walk this path do so because they're out of options. But that's the beauty
found on the narrow path.

Later in 2 Corinthians, Paul said this:

So to keep me from becoming proud, I was given a thorn
in my flesh, a messenger from Satan to torment me and
keep me from becoming proud.

Three different times I begged the Lord to take it
away. Each time he said, "My grace is all you need. My
power works best in weakness." So now I am glad to
boast about my weaknesses, so that the power of Christ
can work through me. That's why I take pleasure in my
weaknesses, and in the insults, hardships, persecutions,

and troubles that I suffer for Christ. For when I am weak,

then I am strong. (2 Cor. 12:7–10 NLT)

I heard the former pastor of Southeast Christian Church, Bob Russell, say one time, "When God has an impossible task to accomplish, he finds an impossible person and breaks them." So, for reasons we don't know, and Paul didn't understand, God allowed the "thorn in his flesh" to torment him to keep him from becoming proud, to help Paul find brokenness. Why? Because: "My power works best in weakness."

To make the journey from perfect to real, you must realize that your brokenness is not weakness. On the contrary, it's the path for you to experience the transformative power of Jesus.

So how do you find this path? That is what we will talk about in the following four chapters. It's a counterintuitive path. It can be a lonely path:

1. You have to let go of people-pleasing.

2. You have to be brutally honest with God.

3. You have to give away your shame.

4. You have to rediscover your identity.

Brokenness and healing are found at the feet of Jesus. Your most remarkable transformation comes as you become desperate for Jesus.

chapter 5

let go of
people-pleasing

living from the approval of God frees us from
living for the approval of people

> "Becoming obsessed with what people think about you is the quickest way
> to forget what God thinks about you."
>
> Craig Groeschel

"We are leaving the church."

Those were the last five words of a lengthy text message from a long-time friend telling me his family was leaving Hope City, the church my wife and I started in 2016. Beyond being a longtime friend, this man and his wife were a part of a small team that formed and launched the church. They were trusted friends and leaders.

I was driving to a meeting when I got the text, and my hands started shaking immediately. I looked in my rearview mirror to see who was behind me and began looking for a place to pull over. He was breaking up with me over a text. He and his wife and their two kids, whom I had dedicated at the church, were leaving the church—and he told me over a text message.

I couldn't believe it. I pulled the car over and called Trisha. She answered the phone, and I started bawling. "Kim and Josh are leaving the church." She was stunned and speechless. "Did you hear me? They are leaving the church," I yelled.

"How do you know," she asked. "Are you sure?"

"HE TEXTED ME. HE SENT ME A TEXT MESSAGE!"

Finally, she said, "Maybe it's a misunderstanding; just give him a call."

I was crying hard at this point. "Okay. I'll call him." I calmed down enough to call, and the phone rang and rang, and then he picked up. In as calm and "pretend okay" voice as I could muster, I said, "Hey, bro. I got your text, and I had to pull the car over to read it, because I thought it said you guys were leaving the church. Am I reading this right?"

It was early 2022, and the conversation he started to have with me was almost the same conversation I'd had with several people who left Hope City during the two years of Covid-19:

> "A lot has changed for us over the last few months."
>
> "Covid has changed things."
>
> "It's not the church. It's us."
>
> "It's not you and Trish. We just need something different."
>
> "We are just ready for a change."
>
> "We think we'll grow more spiritually if we make a change."
>
> "Again, it's not you. It's not Trish. It's not the church."

A year before this text exchange, Trisha and I were out for Valentine's Day. We typically have horrendous experiences on Valentine's Day, so we try to temper our expectations. I'd been having panic attacks, bouts of anxiety, and sleeplessness in ways I'd never struggled with before, but this night felt different. I wasn't feeling well the entire night. My heart was racing, and I couldn't get it to stop. Finally, it got so bad I told Trish I wanted to go home and lie down.

When we got home, I walked upstairs and sat on the bed. Trish asked if I was okay, and I said, "I think I'm having a heart attack. We need to go to the hospital." When we arrived, they did all the standardized tests and took my blood pressure. It was dangerously high. I asked the doctor how bad it was, and his response was, "I'm surprised you aren't having a stroke." So, they completed the initial tests, and I didn't have a heart attack, but they couldn't get my blood pressure down without some heavy sedation.

The doctor gave the medicine some time to work its magic and then came in to explain that I had hypertension and my blood pressure needed to be regulated with medication. Up to this point in my life, I'd been a healthy person. I'd never had surgery or been under anesthesia. Feeling the medication, I didn't realize how relaxed you could be and still be awake. It was like a truth serum. He asked me, "Do you have anything stressful in your life right now?" Tears filled my eyes and leaked down my cheeks, and I explained to him that I was a pastor of a five-year-old church and Covid had been hard on our church and me. We'd recently reopened our building and restarted in-person worship services, but only about 20 percent of our pre-Covid attendance had returned.

Some were watching online, but many decided to leave. Some left because they didn't like our mask mandate. I was "too much of a Democrat." They went to a church that didn't require masks. Some left because they were offended we'd be so reckless to open our building during a pandemic and put lives at risk. I was "too much of a Republican." They were going to watch a more loving, health-conscious church from home.

Some left because I attended a Black Lives Matters rally with my wife, biological son, and two adopted black kids a few weeks after George Floyd's death. I posted a picture of my black kids with the hashtag #blacklivesmatter on Instagram. For some, that was too political, too liberal, too offensive. They wanted a pastor who would value all lives, not just black ones. Others didn't tell me why they were leaving. They just never returned, stopped their online giving, and faded away.

Twelve months into Covid, I developed a disposition: anytime I received an email or text message asking for a meeting, a coffee, or a lunch appointment, I assumed the person was leaving the church.

It had been the most brutal twelve months of my ministry life. The exam room of Urgent Care became a counseling room for a few moments. The doctor patted me on my shoulder and said, "It's been a hard year for many people. I think you need more than this medicine. You need a lifestyle change and counseling."

The next day, I called a counselor and started going to counseling weekly. In my first appointment, I shared with him about Valentine's Day and the doctor's recommendation to see a counselor, to which he replied, "Most pastors I meet with are people pleasers."

I said, "That's what you think I am? You think I'm a people pleaser?"

He said, "No. I don't think you are. I know you are. You need you to think you are."

So, I dug into counseling. I went on blood-pressure medication. I adjusted my diet and started going on walks. Finally, I got to the point where I could admit I was a people pleaser. I was making progress until those five words hit my eyes and heart: "We are leaving the church."

After I got off the phone with Josh, I emailed my counselor. (He wouldn't give me his cell-phone number. Boundaries, or something.) I told him I needed to see him as soon as possible. Thankfully, he emailed back and said he had had a cancellation that afternoon and I could come in at 2:00 p.m.

I walked into his office, sat down, and started crying. He said, "What is going on?"

I said, haltingly, "He's leaving the church."

"Who is?"

"Josh. Josh and his wife, Kim. They are leaving."

He said, "We've talked about this; you can't control when people leave."

I said, "He's leaving me. I can't believe he's leaving me. It's like one of my kids leaving me." And tears and cries just erupted out of me.

He let me sit there and cry for a few minutes. Finally, he stood up and handed me a box of tissues. "You think he's leaving you?"

"Yes. I know he is."

"You need him to go to your church to be friends with him?"

"Well, no, I guess not."

"So you need him to go to your church to feel good about yourself? If he leaves, then that means anyone can leave?"

I said, "If he leaves, it means that everyone at some point will leave."

My counselor said something at that moment that pulled the veil back on my people-pleasing soul: "As long as you need to please people to be whole, you'll never be whole, and you'll use people whether you want to or not."

I thought I'd made so much progress, but my friend leaving the church revealed, "My name is Justin, and I am addicted to people-pleasing."

how to know you're a people pleaser

How do you know if you are a people pleaser? In his book *The People Pleaser's Guide to Loving Others without Losing Yourself,* Dr. Mike Bechtle shared a quiz designed to reveal the degree of people-pleasing you currently practice. Here are his instructions:

Read each question and answer with your immediate response. Don't think too long about your answer. That's especially important if you're a people pleaser, since you've built a pattern of crafting responses to fit what you "should" say. It's critical to be as honest as possible, knowing that the goal is clarity—not impressing others. Circle the appropriate answer for each question.

Do you regularly have anxiety, depression, headaches, stomach issues, or back pain?

Always   Often   Sometimes   Rarely   Never

Do you avoid conflict so no one will criticize you?

Always   Often   Sometimes   Rarely   Never

Do people say you're one of the nicest people they know?

Always   Often   Sometimes   Rarely   Never

Do you keep your negative feelings inside?

Always   Often   Sometimes   Rarely   Never

Do you say yes when you really feel like saying no?

Always   Often   Sometimes   Rarely   Never

Is it hard to imagine standing up for yourself because people might not like you?

Always   Often   Sometimes   Rarely   Never

Do you usually wonder what people are thinking about you?

Always   Often   Sometimes   Rarely   Never

Were you punished for showing anger as a child?

    Always   Often   Sometimes   Rarely   Never

Would you consider yourself a perfectionist?

    Always   Often   Sometimes   Rarely   Never

Do you feel guilty saying no?

    Always   Often   Sometimes   Rarely   Never

Do you avoid journaling for fear someone might read it?

    Always   Often   Sometimes   Rarely   Never

Do you have a hard time asking others for help?

    Always   Often   Sometimes   Rarely   Never

Do you allow visitors to stay longer than they should?

    Always   Often   Sometimes   Rarely   Never

Do you feel hurt when others don't show their appreciation for what you've done?

    Always   Often   Sometimes   Rarely   Never

Do you lie to keep from being rejected or misunderstood by others?

    Always   Often   Sometimes   Rarely   Never

Are you critical of decisions you've made in the past—is it hard to let them go?

    Always   Often   Sometimes   Rarely   Never

Do you bury your feelings?

Always   Often   Sometimes   Rarely   Never

Are you overwhelmed with a never-ending to-do list?

Always   Often   Sometimes   Rarely   Never

Do you have a tough time making decisions on your own?

Always   Often   Sometimes   Rarely   Never

Do you apologize even if you weren't really at fault?

Always   Often   Sometimes   Rarely   Never

Do you feel like you're getting trapped into being a people pleaser, and it's getting worse?

Always   Often   Sometimes   Rarely   Never

When people disagree with you, do you tend to soften your position?

Always   Often   Sometimes   Rarely   Never

Do you compliment people so they'll like you?

Always   Often   Sometimes   Rarely   Never

Do you come to work early or stay late so people will be impressed with you?

Always   Often   Sometimes   Rarely   Never

Do you compare yourself with others?

Always   Often   Sometimes   Rarely   Never

When someone complains about something, do you keep
quiet if you disagree?

    Always   Often   Sometimes   Rarely   Never

Do you only try things when you know you'll succeed?

    Always   Often   Sometimes   Rarely   Never

Is it easier for you to give than to take?

    Always   Often   Sometimes   Rarely   Never

Do you avoid complaining about poor service or quality?

    Always   Often   Sometimes   Rarely   Never

Are you an image-conscious person?

    Always   Often   Sometimes   Rarely   Never

The scoring system starts at 4 points for *Always* and goes down a point with each answer to 0 at *Never*. Here is how Dr. Bechtle categorized the scoring range:

- 91–120 indicates people-pleasing is your identity. It plays a significant role in your emotional
  health. How people perceive you affects how you
  live your life.
- 61–90 is the habit range. You are in the habit of
  people-pleasing but haven't yet made it your
  identity.

- 31–60 is the stage of routine. You have the potential to be unhealthy when it comes to people-pleasing, but you are still in control.
- 0–30 is the healthy range. You may have people-pleasing tendencies, but you have a healthy view of yourself.[1]

What do you do if you score a perfect 120? I'm asking for a friend.

pleasing to people vs. people pleaser

As we choose to let go of people-pleasing, it's essential to note that being a pleasing person isn't bad. We should be pleasing to God. We should try to please others. You can't have a great marriage without pleasing your spouse. You can't have healthy friendships without being an enjoyable person. You can't progress in your career without pleasing your boss or supervisor. Pleasing others isn't wrong. In fact, we are told several times in Scripture to please others:

"Each of us should please our neighbors for their good, to build them up" (Rom. 15:2).

"Do not repay anyone evil for evil. Be careful to do what is right in the eyes of everyone. If it is possible, as far as it depends on you, live at peace with everyone" (Rom. 12:17–18).

"I, too, try to please everyone in everything I do. I don't just do what is best for me; I do what is best for others so that many may be saved. And you should imitate me, just as I imitate Christ" (1 Cor. 10:33–11:1 NLT).

The choice to let go of people-pleasing isn't a declaration of "You do you," without regard for others. There is a healthy aspect of people-pleasing. Part of our humanity is being kind to others. As followers of Jesus, we are called to serve others, to place others' needs ahead of ours. But there is also a point where people-pleasing becomes unhealthy to ourselves and damaging to our relationship with God.

What is the differentiator? How can you know if you are pleasing to people or being a people pleaser?

Motives.

My friend Dr. Derwin Gray defines people-pleasing as "elevating others' opinion of us above God's calling of us."[2]

The motivation for people-pleasing is insecurity. *Merriam-Webster's* defines *insecurity* as "a state or feeling of anxiety, fear, or self-doubt."[3]

When we allow the opinions, thoughts, and beliefs of others to dictate our choices or guide our lives, we start to believe untruths about ourselves and others that keep us from God's best. We can't experience transformation if we are living for the approval of others.

four lies people pleasers believe

How do we accumulate points on Dr. Bechtle's people-pleasers test? If you're like me, it's not all at once. I became predisposed to people-pleasing a little at a time. Over the past few months, I noticed four lies that caused me to elevate the opinion and approval of others above the identity and call God has given me.

"I can be good enough"

The first lie a people pleaser believes is "I can be good enough to be accepted." We all have a desire to belong. It's one of the basic human needs we've identified. We also have a fear of being rejected. We have a fear that we won't be good enough to belong. Maybe for you, you never felt like you belonged in your family. Perhaps you weren't accepted into a specific friend group in high school. Maybe you didn't feel like you belonged at your church. Maybe there are deep wounds connected to your lack of acceptance. You feel like an outsider at work. You question whether God accepts you.

In our quest to be good enough to belong, we need a way to measure ourselves. For many of us, social media is how we compare how we stack up to others. Theodore Roosevelt is the first credited with saying "Comparison is the thief of joy." In our culture, we could substitute that for "Instagram is the thief of joy" or "Social media is the thief of joy."

As you scroll through social media, almost everything you see is the highlight reel of others' lives. Very few people post the lowlights of their lives.

Pastor Shawn Johnson says in his book *Attacking Anxiety*:

> It's almost impossible to spend a significant amount of time on social media and not feel more insecure and unstable. I mean, have you ever spent twenty minutes looking at social media and felt better about your life? Probably not often. Why? Because social media has turned into one big comparison game. And since our normal can't compete with other people's highlight reels, it leaves all of us feeling sad.[4]

When comparison leaves us disappointed in our quest to belong, we become consumed with the opinions of others. We are so insecure in our value that we look to the opinions of others to find our worth. We think our appearance will help us belong—the car we drive, the house we live in, the corner office we earn, the school our kids attend. If we can be good enough, we will fit in.

We can become consumed with what people think of the clothes we wear, the answers we give in class, our performance at work, what someone thinks of a comment we posted on social media. Our need for belonging can cause us to obsess over the thoughts and opinions of others.

What if I told you the people whose opinions we are obsessing over don't even think about us that much?

In an article titled "Research Confirms That No One Is Really Thinking about You," Dr. Deb Knobelman wrote this:

> I used to spend a lot of time worrying about how other people judged me.
>
> What I wore, was it appropriate, did it fit right? Did I say too much? Did I say too little? This person must think I'm too intense. And that person must think I'm not very fun.
>
> And the thoughts were worse at certain times. When I was presenting in a work meeting, or when I was out at a social event. It was so distracting and difficult to stay in the present moment. Because I had a whole inner monologue going on in my head. I assumed every facial expression and every comment from others meant something. And there were always specific themes and beliefs. Universal truths about myself that other people surely thought. I'd hone them and shine them like a pretty little marble and then keep them in my pocket. It was exhausting.

She went on to say:

> Nobody is thinking that much about me. Because we
> mostly think about ourselves.
>   Don't believe it? Do you still think the people around
> you are spending a lot of time thinking about everything
> you do and say? Science disagrees....
>   There's actually scientific evidence that we mostly
> think about ourselves.[5]

Proverbs 29:25 says, "Fear of man will prove to be a snare, but whoever trusts in the LORD is kept safe."

The word translated "snare" in this passage is a Hebrew word used to describe the ring put in a bull's nose to lead him. The picture Solomon offers is that our fear of the opinions of others will lead us around like cattle are led by the nose. But then he provides us with a picture of how to overcome the fear of not being enough for others: "Whoever trusts in the LORD is kept safe."

The word *safe* can also be translated as "secure." The opposite of insecurity is security. When we fear the opinions of others, we are led by insecurity. But when we trust in the Lord, we find security. What I love about this verse is it doesn't say "will be kept safe." It's not in the future tense. It's in the present tense. It's instant. It's immediate. You can find security in the Lord now. God breaks the chain of insecurity in your life when you trust Him.

"my accomplishments gain approval"

The second lie people pleasers believe is "My accomplishments can gain your approval." Did you grow up in an accomplishment-driven home? Your grades may have determined your parents' approval. Your athletic accomplishments may have dictated your value. Perhaps you were told you weren't as smart or as athletic as a sibling. You thought then, and you think now, that if you could only accomplish more, you could earn the approval of your parents, teachers, coaches, boss, or spouse. You could feel validated.

If this describes you, you are on the treadmill of approval. Unfortunately, the harder you run and the faster you sprint, the more worn out you become. No matter how much you accomplish, it's never enough.

Because your accomplishments determine your approval by others, criticism is equated as disapproval. If you receive a critical comment from your boss, your value to the organization is now in question. You wonder what their opinion of you truly is. If your spouse is critical of your choice or behavior, they are really disapproving of you as a person. If a friend says something meant to be constructive criticism about your parenting, you question your friend's commitment to your relationship.

In February 2022, Jeanine Amapola interviewed Olympic gold medalist gymnast Shawn Johnson and her husband, Andrew East, on the *Happy and Healthy* podcast. (This is not the same Shawn Johnson as Pastor Shawn Johnson quoted above. It's just a wild coincidence.) In the interview, Jeanine asked Shawn, "What is something you'd tell your younger self now, looking back?"

Shawn replied, "I would just go back and tell myself, 'Stop trying so hard to please everybody.' I spent years of my life trying to cater my image and my brand and my personality and my clothes and how I talked to society's standards of what they thought was appropriate and what they thought was cool and popular. I got so tired of that."[6]

It struck me that the one thing this world-class athlete, Olympic champion, wife, mom, and social media influencer, if given the chance, would go back and tell her younger self is "Stop trying so hard to please everybody."

I have a bold prediction. You are not going to be a gold-medal-winning Olympic gymnast. That is an accomplishment that you will never have. So, I'm setting you free from that expectation. But even a gold-medal-winning Olympic gymnast couldn't accomplish enough to feel like everyone approved of her.

The apostle Paul walked the tightrope of pursuing God's approval and not being led by the people's approval. Look what he said in 1 Thessalonians 2:4:

> For we speak as messengers approved by God to be entrusted with the Good News. Our purpose is to please God, not people. He alone examines the motives of our hearts. (NLT)

His value as a messenger of the Good News was determined by God's approval, not the opinions of others. Your value as a husband, wife, father, or mother comes from your approval by God. Your value as an employee or employer comes from your approval by God. Your value as a friend comes from your approval by God.

I love what Paul said next: "God alone examines the motives of our hearts." Paul didn't address our behavior as people pleasers. Instead, he said this is a heart issue. The motives of your heart determine where you find your value.

"I can earn love"

The third lie people pleasers believe is "My performance will earn your love." One of the things my counselor helped me work through after Kim and Josh left Hope City was my motive for becoming a pastor. The first and most compelling reason I became a pastor was that I felt God called me to vocational ministry. I believe the church is the hope of the world, and I want to spend the best years of my life helping people find hope and follow Jesus. That is my calling. My second motivation to serve God in pastoral ministry is that I love people. I love seeing life transformation in people. I love seeing marriages restored. I love seeing relationships reconciled. I love seeing people understand the grace of God for the first time. I love people.

When I started counseling during Covid, those were the two reasons I gave my counselor for why I became a pastor. But when Kim and Josh left the church, I discovered a third reason I became a pastor.

I need people to love me.

Love from others is a basic human need. In and of itself, love from others isn't unhealthy; it's essential. But when you equate your performance as a mom, friend, employee, spouse, or pastor with winning or gaining love from others, it goes beyond unhealthy and becomes toxic.

For over twenty years of vocational ministry, I lived with an unknown equation: my performance as a pastor would equate to love from others. Of course, I wanted people to fall in love with Jesus, but I *needed* them to love me.

If my sermons were deep enough, our services were engaging enough, our worship was edgy enough, our kids' ministry was good enough, then more people would come to church, and in the process of loving Jesus, they would also love me.

The intensity and complexity of Covid exposed this broken part of my heart. As I worked through this with my counselor, I read a few verses in the gospel of John that I knew I'd read before but had never truly seen before.

> Many people did believe in him, however, including some
> of the Jewish leaders. But they wouldn't admit it for fear

that the Pharisees would expel them from the synagogue.

For they loved human praise more than the praise of God.

(John 12:42–43 NLT)

Jesus was on His way to the cross. It was Passion Week, and He was about to wash the disciples' feet. Jesus had taught as one who had authority. He had healed the sick and brought sight to the blind. The Jewish leaders had seen all the miracles and heard all the teachings of the kingdom of God. John said they did believe in Him, but their fear kept them from admitting it.

I read that verse and thought, *How could they be so driven by the opinion and approval of others?* Then the next verse cut deep into my heart: "For they loved human praise more than the praise of God."

"my efforts meet all expectations"

The final lie people pleasers believe is "My effort can meet everyone's expectations."

One of the first things publishers tell new authors during book-release week is "Don't read the Amazon reviews." When Trish and I released *Beyond Ordinary* in 2013, it was very personal. We wrote in a memoir style, so our story was central to the book's message. We shared vulnerable and intimate moments of our marriage, our relationship with God, our personal and collective failures that led to my affair, and the implosion of our marriage.

When an affair is revealed or goes public, it is a shock to people on the outside. But when a marriage shatters publicly, it's been struggling privately for quite a while. We wanted to give the reader insight into the private struggle of our marriage so they could see their marriage in our story and make adjustments to avoid the pain we experienced.

The book's last few chapters share the process we went through to find healing and the restoration we are living in, even as I write this chapter today. In our minds, the story of *Beyond Ordinary* was a raw and honest look into the life of a couple who started with great intentions, lost our way, and then, by God's grace, found redemption, healing, and a new beginning.

We knew the principles we shared in the book worked; they worked for us. We knew the danger signs we listed in the book were true; we'd talked to hundreds of couples who affirmed each pitfall. We trusted the content was strong, because after we sent the manuscript out to pastors, movement leaders, and Christian influencers for endorsements, the private conversations and emails we received back were so encouraging and affirming.

We sent the manuscript to Gary Thomas. He is the author of many books, but his best known is *Sacred Marriage*. We had some mutual friends, but we'd never met. We asked Gary to read *Beyond Ordinary* and offer an endorsement if he believed in the book's message. A few weeks after we sent the manuscript, I got a text message from a number I didn't recognize. It was from Gary: "I'm in Nashville speaking at a conference. Do you and Trisha have time for lunch?" For the author of *Sacred Marriage*, I am clearing my calendar.

We were sitting at lunch with Gary Thomas, author of the most influential books I've ever read on marriage, and he said, "You guys can be honest with me. Who was your ghostwriter on *Beyond Ordinary*?"

Trish and I looked at each other, a little confused. Trish said, "There wasn't a ghostwriter. We wrote every word of the book."

I said, "What makes you think we have a ghostwriter?"

He said, "The story is so compelling, and the content is so good; I just figured you must have a ghostwriter. Please know I am giving you both a huge compliment."

It was one of those moments that I'll never forget. It would be like Steph Curry complimenting my jump shot. An author of Gary's stature believing in us and our book was terrific. Gary believed in us so much that he wrote the foreword to *Beyond Ordinary.*

I wish I could have remembered that feeling and encouragement during the book's release a few months later. As more people read *Beyond Ordinary*, we saw that Amazon reviews were being posted. Despite the publisher's advice, I wanted the validation I was sure I would find in the reviews. As of the writing of this chapter, our book has 532 Amazon reviews, and 90 percent of them are four- and five-star reviews. That should shine brightly compared to the 3 percent of one-star reviews. But for a few weeks after the book was released, the one-star reviews dominated my heart. Here are a few of my "favorites":

> There are literally hundreds of books you should be reading as a couple before getting to this one.... The pride that will leap off the pages of this book will make you question the salvation of its authors and make you pity the children that are largely neglected throughout. Perhaps the most saddening aspect is the dozens of well-meaning Christians who have been hoodwinked by this slick-talking salesman and have put their own reputations and ministries at stake to support him and continue to offer him a seat at the table even after he has disqualified himself. In the end you have a wife who continues to admit to hating God and being angry with Him for the sins of her broken husband while enabling his behavior and a husband who ignores his own pride even as he revels in it

and continues to seek a life as a pastor despite not knowing even basic doctrine or theology.

I didn't get past the first third of the book. I got bored
hearing their whining about each other.

Clearly, this book was written to promote the couple's
church and speaking engagements, but the book should
be titled "the life of an arrogant a-hole." I honestly
feel sorry for Trisha. Her husband is an arrogant, self-
important adulterer with a God complex. I know this
book is about helping or saving marriages, but I truly
feel it was just a book about how great Justin is.... In
short, if you are looking for a book with actual marriage
advice, this is not it. In fact, I got so sick of the BS I
skipped to the last several chapters ... it never got any
better. I know that there is a lot to be learned from our
struggles in marriage, but the only thing I learned from
this book is what a jerk Justin is.[7]

Again, we received 90 percent four- and five-star reviews. Gary
Thomas told us how compelling the book was and how strong the content was, and I allowed these three reviews and the 3 percent of one-star
reviews to dominate my heart for weeks. I started to question my heart,
motives, and calling. I wondered if we should stop sharing our story and
stop doing marriage conferences. Had I missed God's design for me? Were
these people right?

> Living from the approval of
> God frees you from living for
> the approval of people.

At lunch with my good friend Steven one day, I pulled out my phone and started reading him some of the one-star reviews. He said, "Justin, why would you allow the voice of a few people that don't know you, will never meet you, and have little to no influence in this world impact how you feel about yourself or the message and ministry God has given you?"

How much of my life have I sacrificed approval from God by seeking the praise of people? What about you? Are you living your life to get five-star reviews from others rather than living in the five-star reviews you have from God? Do you see the validation from others tied to your production and your effort? Your performance might earn a form of love from others, but it's not real love. When love is based on what we do, it diminishes who we are.

letting go of people-pleasing

If you want to shift from being perfect to being real, you must let go of people-pleasing. In Christ:

> You are accepted.
> You are loved.
> You do belong.
> You are secure.

If my pep talk doesn't do it for you, look at what Paul said in Galatians 1:10:

> Obviously, I'm not trying to win the approval of people,
> but of God. If pleasing people were my goal, I would not
> be Christ's servant. (NLT)

Living from the approval of God frees you from living for the approval of people. You can let go of people-pleasing.

be brutally
honest with God

God can handle your hurts; He can understand your
doubts, but He doesn't heal your heart until you're honest

"Lord, if you had been here, my brother would not have died."

Martha, sister of Lazarus

One of the first things longtime residents of Nashville, Tennessee, share with you when you first move to the city is how to react when you see celebrities in the wild. These instructions are crucial for starstruck fanboys like me, who revel in meeting famous people.

Here is a brief summary of how to respond when sighting famous people: Don't flinch. Don't respond. Don't ask for an autograph. Don't point. Don't shriek like a middle schooler. Don't react. Don't stare. Don't draw attention.

Because I was one of the pastors of a growing and influential church in the heart of Music City, these instructions were essential to my vocation and the depth of public embarrassment I could cause my family. From my first week on staff at Cross Point, I started meeting people I'd only seen on TV or heard on the radio. As a result, my wife and kids routinely reminded me not to make a scene if we saw a music artist or television personality in public. Most of the time, it worked.

I showed great self-control a few weeks after we moved to Nashville when, on a date day, I went to pay our bill at the Pancake Pantry. As I was standing in line, the couple in front of me turned to leave. I didn't say anything to Vince Gill and Amy Grant and acted like I saw them daily.

I demonstrated restraint when I walked into Sam's Club and saw a woman who looked like Faith Hill. I dismissed it, because I assumed Faith Hill would be a Costco person. However, when I pulled my membership card from my wallet, the Sam's Club employee said, "You just walked past Faith Hill."

"No big deal," I think I said.

I moderately embarrassed my family when I pointed at and started saying in a loud voice, "There's Michael Tait. There's Michael Tait!" as we walked through the CoolSprings mall. They dispersed rapidly in humiliation. You get me if you are a DC Talk fan from the early '90s. My family isn't as big of a Jesus Freak as I am.

The good news is that the longer we lived in Nashville, the more I met and got to know some country and Christian music artists and started seeing them as normal people. It was a joy to pastor and befriend a number of people in the music industry.

Several people of influence started attending the church a few years into my time at Cross Point. As a staff, we knew we must continue to be a safe and welcoming place for anyone, including recognizable musicians and artists. Most of the time, artists would slip in and slip out. Occasionally, fans would recognize and approach them in the lobby. We did our best to prevent this from happening.

One Sunday, during the middle of a worship set, an entourage of three or four people came into the back of the auditorium. The service was already full, so a few staff were at the back of the room helping people find seats. I went up to the group and told them that if they could wait for a few minutes, I could help them find a seat when the song ended. It didn't take long for me to realize I was talking to Taylor Swift.

At this point, I'd been in Nashville for a few years and was no longer a new person. I didn't flinch. After the song ended, I helped them find seats. Some artists can slip in and out of a room and not be noticed. Not this artist. Taylor's presence spread across the room to every pre-teen girl by the end of the message. We had several people scheduled to be baptized to close the service. Our worship pastor asked the congregation to stand and sing as people were being baptized. He invited anyone who felt prompted to be spontaneously baptized to come forward; we had extra shorts and T-shirts and could accommodate anyone feeling God lead in that direction.

There was a ton of movement. People started walking past others in the aisles, and as the music began, people continued going forward. I was standing next to our executive director, and she realized people weren't coming forward to be baptized; they were coming down to Taylor's section to ask her for autographs during the baptisms.

Our executive director spent years in the music industry before coming on staff, so she handled the situation beautifully and escorted Taylor and her friends out the side door and into the staff offices.

Some weeks later, I was speaking, and a few minutes before the service started, our executive director told me that she had received a text from one of Taylor's people that she was coming to the service that morning. She would come in a different entrance, be seated after the service began, and hang out in the office area after the service until everyone left.

The service ended, the crowd left, and it was just staff and staff families, Taylor Swift, and a few of her friends in the building. We were walking out, and the Nashville campus pastor's girls were talking to Taylor and soaking up the moment. At that time, I didn't have a daughter, so I couldn't conceptualize how big of a moment this was for four girls who idolized Taylor.

I approached Taylor and thanked her for allowing us to help her get in and out of the church without people asking for autographs. I said, "I only have one of my kids at this service, my twelve-year-old son, Elijah. I'd love to introduce you." I yelled for Elijah to come over, and when he did, I said, "Elijah, this is Taylor Swift."

He didn't miss a beat. He reached out his hand to shake her hand and said, "Hi, Taylor. I'm Elijah. I don't listen to your music." He turned and went back to the lobby and started playing with his friends again.

I don't remember what happened after that. I blacked out. There is honesty, and there is brutal honesty. Elijah moved past courtesy and right into authenticity. (Don't worry. I'm pretty sure Taylor's self-confidence survived the experience.)

The church culture I grew up in focused on being polite and minding your manners with God, not being honest with Him. Your relationship with God was something to be managed and groomed. God was omniscient and omnipotent and should be revered and feared. Those things are theologically accurate. The Pharisees were theologically correct too, but relationally misguided. They knew God's doctrine, but missed God's heart.

The problem is relationships don't grow by being managed. Relationships grow through honesty, sometimes brutal honesty. If we can't be honest with God about our hurts, doubts, disappointments, questions, sorrows, frustrations, and anger, how deep of a relationship can we have with Him? If we can't trust God with the most fragile, intimate, and vulnerable parts of our hearts, how is He an omniscient, omnipotent God?

growth through authenticity

Our relationships can only grow to the extent we're known. If we don't believe God can fully know us, we'll consistently withhold parts of our hearts from Him, and those portions of our lives will remain unchanged and unhealed.

As you look throughout the Scriptures, you see respect, honor, and fear of God. God's infinite power should be admired and revered. But you also see vulnerability and brutal honesty in every person with a personal relationship with God. Those who followed God closest felt the most comfortable questioning, doubting, complaining, crying out, and admitting weakness to Him.

The people who knew Jesus best acknowledged His deity, but they didn't allow that to prevent them from being authentic with Him. Those who loved Jesus most had the most transparent conversations with Him. Worship and doubt aren't mutually exclusive; they can exist in the same relationship. Love and disappointment can be equally expressed to Jesus. Belief in Jesus and questioning of Jesus were welcomed by Jesus.

Mary, Martha, and Lazarus

The gospel of John chapter 11 begins with:

> Now a man named Lazarus was sick. He was from Bethany, the village of Mary and her sister Martha. (This Mary, whose brother Lazarus now lay sick, was the same one who poured perfume on the Lord and wiped his feet with her hair.) So the sisters sent word to Jesus, "Lord, the one you love is sick." (John 11:1–3)

These three verses give substantial insight into Jesus' relationship with this family. Lazarus is mentioned for the first time here, and John didn't expect the readers to know who Lazarus was, so he qualified his relationship with Jesus. However, we can assume, based on how John referred to Mary and Martha, they were well-known to those who followed Jesus. John said that Lazarus was from Bethany and was the brother of Mary and Martha.

> Those who followed God closest felt the most comfortable questioning, complaining, crying out, and admitting weakness to Him.

John wanted the reader to know the depth of Jesus' relationship with this family. There was devotion from this family to Jesus. Mary, Martha, and Lazarus had a deep love for Jesus. Jesus had a history with this family.

We don't know how long Lazarus was ill. We don't see the process Mary and Martha went through to help Lazarus overcome the illness. But at some point, they realized that the only hope Lazarus had was Jesus. So, they sent a messenger to find Jesus and give Him this message: "Lord, the one you love is sick." This was a message of desperation and anticipation. They needed a miracle, and they expected a miracle.

The medicine wasn't working. The doctors didn't have any answers. Everyone had done all they could do. Jesus was their only hope. Have you ever prayed a prayer of desperation? "Lord, my marriage needs a miracle." "Lord, the cancer is back; we need a miracle." "Lord, we are out of money; this round of chemo has to work." "Lord, my company is downsizing; I need a miracle."

You are desperate and anticipate a miracle.

Throughout his gospel, John referred to himself as the "disciple Jesus loved." It was not only a term of endearment but also a statement of proximity to the heart of Jesus. Mary and Martha sent someone to tell Jesus that one of His best friends was sick. This wasn't a superficial relationship. There was history and depth in that statement: "Lord, the one you love is sick."

Mary and Martha reminded Jesus how much He loved Lazarus, because they believed Jesus could heal Lazarus. It's easy to equate God's love with God's blessing, so they thought if they could remind Jesus how much He loved Lazarus, then Jesus would do what they wanted Him to do. "The one you love is sick."

"When he heard this, Jesus said, 'This sickness will not end in death. No, it is for God's glory so that God's Son may be glorified through it'" (John 11:4).

In this verse, we see something bigger going on than just the health of Lazarus. Jesus was concerned about Lazarus' illness, but He was most concerned with God's glory. On our journey to being real, we must recognize that God's silence doesn't mean His absence. His delay in answering our prayers doesn't mean His denial of the answer to our prayers.

"Jesus loved Martha, her sister, and Lazarus. Yet, when Jesus heard that Lazarus was sick, he stayed where he was for two more days" (John 11:5–6 GW).

Jesus loved Mary. He loved Martha. He loved Lazarus. YET He stayed two more days. I'm sure you've experienced a YET moment with God.

> You prayed for God to save your marriage, YET your spouse left anyway.
> You asked God to heal a loved one, YET they still passed away.

You're doing your best to honor God with your finances, YET you still lost your job.

You've repeatedly told God how much you want to be married, YET you are still single.

You've prayed for God to protect your pregnancies, YET you've had miscarriages.

That word *yet* is more about God's glory than His love for us. Hurts, pains, and loss sometimes make no sense on this side of heaven.

I love what theologian Colin Kruse said about this passage:

> The sisters' implied request to Jesus to come and heal their brother was based upon his love for Lazarus (3). In 11:5 the evangelist reiterates Jesus' love for Lazarus and his sisters. This shows that Jesus' failure to respond in the normal way, staying where he was for two more days, was not due to any lack of love for either Lazarus, who was on the verge of death, or his sisters, who had sent the urgent request for help. The NIV translation "yet when he heard," which implies that Jesus' delay was somehow at odds with his love for them, is misleading. The original (*hōs oun ēkousen*) should be rendered "so when he heard" (as in the RSV), which shows that Jesus' delay was not at odds with his love, but motivated by it.[1]

John wanted us to know that what was about to happen wasn't a reflection of Jesus' love for this family. He loved them, yet He stayed where He was for two more days. The trials or wounds you've endured aren't a reflection of God's love, but they can reflect God's glory.

> After he had said this, he went on to tell them, "Our friend Lazarus has fallen asleep; but I am going there to wake him up."
>
> His disciples replied, "Lord, if he sleeps, he will get better." Jesus had been speaking of his death, but his disciples thought he meant natural sleep.
>
> So then he told them plainly, "Lazarus is dead, and for your sake I am glad I was not there, so that you may believe. But let us go to him."
>
> Then Thomas (also known as Didymus) said to the rest of the disciples, "Let us also go, that we may die with him." (John 11:11–16)

Lazarus died, and the disciples didn't understand. This verse gives me hope as a follower of Jesus. They traveled with Jesus. They saw Jesus do miracles, yet they didn't get what Jesus was saying. So Jesus told them plainly, "Lazarus is dead." I feel this verse, deep in my relationship with God—just make it plain to me, Jesus.

Jesus and the disciples made the two-day journey back to Bethany. It was Jewish custom in the first century to have thirty days of mourning. Four days after the death of Lazarus, we can assume friends and family were still gathered at the house. Word got back to those at the house that Jesus was on His way to Bethany.

We all respond differently to loss. Likewise, we react differently to trauma. Within a few days, Lazarus got sick, Jesus was informed, Jesus didn't show up in time, and Lazarus died. This was a tragic and traumatic situation for Lazarus' friends and family. Mary and Martha responded in two very different ways. Their reactions give us two examples of brutal honesty with God for our journey from being perfect to being real.

> The trials or wounds you've endured aren't a reflection of God's love, but they can reflect God's glory.

"When Martha heard that Jesus was coming, she went out to meet him, but Mary stayed at home" (John 11:20).

be where you are, not where you think you should be

When difficult or devastating circumstances occur in our lives, we can get lost in our own distorted spiritual beliefs. We expect to get it together or have it figured out. If we experience doubt, hurt, sorrow, and distance with God, we might think these are bad things to get over rather than a means by which God will grow our faith and deepen our relationship with Him. We think denying these emotions makes us more spiritual. We shame ourselves, or the Church convinces us that minimizing these realities will maximize our faith. Slowly and subtly, we choose inauthenticity over being real.

How did Martha respond to this trauma? She ran to Jesus. She immediately left to meet Jesus when she heard He was close. For some of us, that is our honest and natural reaction. You experience the loss of a job or the death of a loved one, and you run to Jesus. A relationship ends, or an unexpected diagnosis is given, and that circumstance moves you toward Jesus.

I have a good friend named Ted who was just diagnosed with cancer. He is sixty years old, in excellent health otherwise, never smoked, and has stage-four tongue cancer. Ted served as the chairman of our board at Hope City, and he and his wife, Cheryl, encouraged us and lifted us up so much during the months of Covid. His diagnosis was devastating news to Trish and me. Ted is faithful, kind, and generous. He loves Jesus and uses his influence to point others to Him.

I sent Ted a text and told him how sorry I was for the diagnosis and how difficult this season must be. I asked him if I could do anything for Cheryl or him. This was his response:

> I promised God I would not waste the cancer. I think his plan is for me to go through this, then offer encouragement to others facing the same thing in the future. I plan to do just that.

Ted is running to Jesus in this situation. It's not a facade or an act. A few weeks ago, I performed a wedding for a couple in Ted and Cheryl's small group. Ted was there. He was nine rounds into thirty-two rounds of radiation and three of seven rounds into chemotherapy. While his treatment was taking a toll on his body and stamina, it only strengthened his faith. His proximity to Jesus was close. His intimacy with his heavenly Father was real. He meets Jesus at every radiation treatment and every chemotherapy session.

Maybe that describes your relationship with God. When things hit the fan, and life spins out of control in ways that bring heartache or devastation, running to Jesus is your first response, not your last resort.

Martha ran to Jesus. But did you see how Mary responded to the arrival of Jesus? "Mary stayed at home." Mary needed some space. Mary was hurt and disappointed and sad and frustrated. She had more questions than answers.

John wanted us to know details about Mary as he recounted the story of Lazarus. In verse 2, he said, "This Mary, whose brother Lazarus now lay sick, was the same one who poured perfume on the Lord and wiped his feet with her hair" (John 11:2).

This was the dinner-party-crashing Mary. This was the Mary from Luke 7. This was the Mary who overcame public opinion and people-pleasing to be at the feet of Jesus. Luke told us another detail about this Mary, the sister of Martha and Lazarus: "Her sister, Mary, sat at the Lord's feet, listening to what he taught" (Luke 10:39 NLT).

Mary was no stranger to being at the feet of Jesus. She washed Jesus' feet with her tears, wiped them with her hair, and anointed them with an alabaster jar of perfume. When Martha was distracted trying to make a meal and clean the house, Mary sat at the feet of Jesus and soaked up His teaching.

But now, after the death of her brother, she couldn't be in the presence of Jesus, much less at His feet. She needed time. She needed space. She needed distance.

In June 2009, I got a call from my mom, asking if she could spend the afternoon with me. Trish was out of town with the older two boys, and it was just me and Isaiah for the weekend. We had no plans, so I invited my mom to our house to hang out.

From the time she arrived, I knew something was off. I didn't know what, but she wasn't acting like herself. A few months before, my mom and dad had finalized their divorce after thirty-six years of marriage. My dad had lived a secret life of sexual addiction that came to light and ended their relationship. I knew how much my mom had been through and, at first, just attributed her demeanor to the pain of her own situation. As she prepared to leave, she asked if we could sit down and talk. She had a bag with her and became very emotional. We both sat down on the couch, and she took a Bible out of her bag.

She said, "The past few months have been some of the most difficult of my entire life. We have spent them encouraging your dad to be a man of truth. To be honest. To live with integrity. The more I have gone after your dad to tell the truth, the more God has convicted me of choices I have made to not be a person of truth. One of the things God has laid on my heart is our relationship. I am going to tell you right now, Justin, that I am laying our relationship on the altar. I am willing to sacrifice our relationship to do what is right and to be a person of truth." With that statement, she opened the Bible to Genesis 22, where the story of Abraham taking Isaac up the mountain and putting him on the altar is recorded.

I'm a hypochondriac, so at this point, I wasn't hearing anything my mom was saying. I was thinking, *She is going to sacrifice me? Do I have a deadly disease that she hasn't told me about? I wonder how advanced it is? I wonder how much time I have left? If I were to die, where would they bury me? We haven't even bought a cemetery plot yet! I hope it isn't a painful death. I'm really too young to die!* I know, I have serious issues, but that was my thought process. After I snapped out of it, my mom got to the point of why she was there.

She said, "You know that your dad and I got married fifteen days after you were born. I got pregnant with you out of wedlock." I nodded. "What you don't know and what I have been lying to you about for the past thirty-six years is that when I met your dad, I was eight months pregnant with you. Your dad is not your real dad. Your dad adopted you when you were a toddler. He is your adoptive father, not your biological father."

My head started spinning. She could have told me I was from Mars and it would have made more sense to me than what she was saying. I don't remember much of what else she said, but I do remember asking her to leave. As soon as she was in the car, I called Trisha and told her of the bomb that was just dropped on me. She couldn't make any more sense of it than I could.

I'd love to tell you my response was to run to Jesus. But most of the following year, I needed distance from God. I was disoriented and confused. I needed time to process my identity. I needed distance to understand how to relate to God as a "Father" when my earthly father and mother had so deeply wounded me. I needed space. If I'm honest, I felt guilty about distancing myself from God. I felt like I wasn't being a good Christian; I wasn't a spiritual leader.

I learned that year that being honest about where I was in my relationship with God was the only thing that allowed me to go deeper in my relationship with God. So, if you are processing wounds, trauma, or pain in your life, and you don't feel like running to Jesus, you feel like staying at the house like Mary did, that is okay.

Being at a distance from Jesus doesn't mean you have weak faith; it means your faith needs time to overcome the distance you're experiencing. God can't close the gap if we're not honest about it. It's okay to be where you are, not where you think you should be.

pray what you feel, not what you think you should pray

John gave us insight into the relational intimacy that people who followed Jesus had with Jesus. What we see throughout the account of the death and resurrection of Lazarus is that Jesus wasn't looking for dutiful soldiers; He wanted to be in a relationship with real people. Jesus was secure enough for us to be honest with Him. You can be brutally honest with Jesus.

be honest with Jesus about your doubts

Jesus and His disciples had been doing ministry in Jerusalem, where He upset the religious elite, who then tried to kill Him. So, Jesus and the disciples left Jerusalem and were doing ministry outside the city when Lazarus became sick and died.

> "Lazarus is dead, and for your sake I am glad I was not there, so that you may believe. But let us go to him."
> Then Thomas (also known as Didymus) said to the rest of the disciples, "Let us also go, that we may die with him." (John 11:14–16)

At least one of the disciples wasn't excited about returning to Jerusalem. Do you have anyone in your life who is a "worst-case-scenario person"? No matter what is going on, they always think of the worst possible outcome. They assume things are going to be bad, no matter what. While I consider myself an optimist, my wife says that I'm a worst-case-scenario person.

Jesus told the disciples that Lazarus was dead, and Thomas didn't care about Lazarus or his family; instead, he sarcastically said back to Jesus,

"Let's go back to Jerusalem so we can die with him." Jesus was glad He wasn't there so the disciple's faith would grow, but Thomas had no belief in Jesus coming through in any way in this situation. The only thing that was growing for Thomas was his doubt. But I love this verse because Thomas, a disciple of Jesus, didn't hesitate to say what he felt. He was that comfortable around Jesus.

Later in John's gospel, after the resurrection of Jesus, the disciples were gathered in a room when Jesus appeared to them. Thomas was not with them, so the disciples told him of their encounter with Jesus.

> Now Thomas (also known as Didymus), one of the Twelve, was not with the disciples when Jesus came. So the other disciples told him, "We have seen the Lord!"
> But he said to them, "Unless I see the nail marks in his hands and put my finger where the nails were, and put my hand into his side, I will not believe." (John 20:24–25)

Thomas had traveled with Jesus. He'd seen Him perform miracles and bring Lazarus back from the dead. His closest friends were telling him they had seen the Lord, and he doubted. Here is the best part of the story:

> A week later his disciples were in the house again, and Thomas was with them. Though the doors were locked, Jesus came and stood among them and said, "Peace be with you!" Then he said to Thomas, "Put your finger here; see my hands. Reach out your hand and put it into my side. Stop doubting and believe." (John 20:26–27)

Jesus showed up, and He met Thomas in his doubt. He invited Thomas to touch Him. He didn't shame him for doubting. He met him in his doubt. He went to Thomas. Thomas was brave enough to say what he felt, not what he thought he should feel.

Are there honest prayers you need to permit yourself to pray? Are you sanitizing your prayer life, trying not to offend God? You can be brutally honest with God about your doubts.

be honest with Jesus about your hurts

Martha ran to Jesus. Jesus wasn't four hours late. He was four days late. They had sent word for Him with time to spare. Lazarus didn't have to die. Jesus could have been there. He could have done something. Martha had four days to rehearse this speech. She had four days to think about what she would say to Jesus when she saw Him again.

"'Lord,' Martha said to Jesus, 'if you had been here, my brother would not have died'" (John 11:21).

If You had been here, Jesus. If You had shown up, this wouldn't have happened. So often, when we experience trauma or hurt, what is most challenging in our relationship with God isn't our belief that God couldn't intervene; we believe that He could have, and He chose not to.

In January 2022, our facility lease for Hope City Church expired. We had rented space from an older church whose attendance had declined over the years. Their congregation met in the gym, and we rented their auditorium, lobby, and children's wing. We moved into their building in December 2019, about eight weeks before the Covid-19 shutdown, giving us room to grow and gain strong momentum. Then Covid hit and changed everything.

Before shutting down for Covid, we were a church of over 600 people. Even though we went back to in-person services in October 2020, our weekly attendance average, now two years later, was about 70. Our giving, which held strong for most of 2020, steadily declined in 2021, and we had to lay off staff at the end of the year. I met with each of our small groups at the beginning of 2022, explained the situation to them, and told them that if our attendance and giving didn't increase between January and Easter, we'd have some tough decisions to make.

In February, we were informed the church we rented from subleased our space to a homeschool co-op. We had until Easter to find another place to meet. We'd been in a yearlong search for our long-term home, and this news intensified our search.

In March 2022, we thought we had found a great facility from a location and space standpoint, but the property owner rejected our offer. So we called an emergency board meeting to discuss our options. Unfortunately, as our discussion progressed, it became apparent we didn't have a lot of options.

One of our board members said, "As much as it hurts to say this, maybe we should close the church." As a founding pastor and leader, I can't describe how painful that was to hear. I looked up from the financial statement I was staring at and saw tears in Trisha's eyes. I glanced around the table, and each board member felt the same way.

April 24, 2022, was the last Sunday of Hope City Church. We announced the closing of the church on April 10. The following Sunday was Easter, and we had 317 in attendance. Over 250 people attended our final service. By God's grace, I had a counseling session scheduled for the Thursday following our last Sunday.

That Thursday session was intense. I was so hurt and so raw. I was upset that our attendance was so high the last two weeks. I kept telling my counselor, "If those people had been there the past year, we wouldn't have closed."

About halfway through our session, my counselor asked me, "Who are you really mad at?"

I said, "I guess I'm mad at myself for failing."

He said, "Did you do everything you could? Did you do your best? Did you give everything you had to help the church succeed?"

"Yes, I did," I replied.

"So then you didn't fail."

"Who failed you?" he pressed.

I said, "The people that left?"

"Okay, I'll give you that, but who really failed you?"

I took a deep breath. "God. God failed me. God called me to do this, only to drop-kick me in the end. God could have intervened. He could have provided a building. He could have shown up. I gave everything and God failed me. I'm so angry with God." Tears and convulsing cries ensued.

"Now we have a starting point. You can't find healing until you're honest about where you are," he said.

Martha got straight to the point. "If you would have been here, we wouldn't be hurting like this, Jesus." After she confronted Jesus, she went back to get Mary. Mary then decided to leave the house and meet Jesus.

"When Mary reached the place where Jesus was and saw him, she fell at his feet and said, 'Lord, if you had been here, my brother would not have died'" (John 11:32).

This verse is incredible. Where did Mary go? She fell at His feet. The distance was removed. Her desire to be near Jesus had become greater than her anger toward Him. She was back in close proximity to Jesus. But she felt free to express her hurt. "If you'd been here, Jesus, my brother would not have died." Mary said in person what she had felt at a distance.

Maybe you find yourself at the feet of Jesus, but to heal, you need to express your hurts. "If You had been there, Jesus, my baby wouldn't have died. If You had been there, Jesus, my marriage wouldn't have ended. If You had been there, Jesus, I wouldn't have been abused. If You had been there, Jesus, my dad wouldn't have left." Be honest with Jesus about your hurts. Be open with Him about your wounds. Be vulnerable with Him about your pain. Fall at His feet, and pour out your heart.

be honest with Jesus about your sorrow

When you choose to be honest with Jesus about your doubts and your hurts, you discover that He meets you in your doubts and empathizes with your hurts. Mary and Martha went to Jesus and were vulnerable with Him, and they shared their sorrow with their Savior.

That honesty and vulnerability moves the heart of Jesus.

"When Jesus saw her weeping, and the Jews who had come along with her also weeping, he was deeply moved in spirit and troubled. 'Where have you laid him?' he asked. 'Come and see, Lord,' they replied. Jesus wept. Then the Jews said, 'See how he loved him!'" (John 11:33–36).

Many of us have adopted a version of Christianity that doesn't allow for sorrow or sadness. If you are sad or experience grief, you need to get over it or push through it. You can't be a person of both great faith and deep sadness.

Not only does Jesus not look down on you for feeling sad or experiencing sorrow, but our expression of sadness to Him moves His heart. Hebrews 4:15 says that Jesus empathizes with us. *Psychology Today* defines *empathy* as "the ability to recognize, understand, and share the thoughts and feelings of another."[2]

Jesus doesn't just understand your feelings; He feels what you are feeling. You can bring Jesus your doubts because He'll meet you in them. You can bring Jesus your hurts because He understands your pain. You can bring Him your sorrow because He shares it with you.

To move from perfect to real, you must be brutally honest with God. Jesus can handle your hurts; He can understand your doubts, but He can't heal your heart until you're honest.

chapter 7

give away your shame

shame diminishes God's grace and robs you of God's best

> *"We all experience shame. We're all afraid to talk about it. And, the less we talk about it, the more we have it."*
>
> Brené Brown, *Daring Greatly*

Before Trisha and I wrote the book *Beyond Ordinary: When a Good Marriage Just Isn't Good Enough*, we shared our story on our website, refineus.org. We did and continue to do our best to be open and honest about our mistakes, choices we regret, and the restoration and redemption God brought to our relationship. But we go first, so others feel permission to go second.

As we shared our story online, we began to get requests to speak and share our testimony at churches all over the country. So, in the early days of RefineUs, we would travel to a church, share our testimony on a Sunday morning, and then return home.

One Sunday, we were in Tampa, Florida, and as we shared our story, we heard cries and sobs from the congregation. It was heavy. We finished the second service, talked to people at the door, and then started home. About thirty minutes into our trip home, Trisha said, "I don't want to do this anymore."

I said, "Okay. If you don't want to share our story, we don't have to share our story."

She said, "No, that's not what I mean. We go into these churches, and all these unsuspecting people come that day not knowing what we are about to share. We talk about sexual brokenness, hiddenness, and unforgiveness. Then, in the last five minutes of the message, we say, 'But God healed us, and we're doing great today. So, let's close in prayer.' I don't want to do that anymore. I want to equip people to experience God's best for their marriage, not just tell them how ours imploded."

A few hours later, I got a text message from a friend from college. He said, "I heard you guys spoke at Danny's church in Tampa today. We'd love for you guys to do a marriage conference for us in October. Talk it over with Trish and let me know."

I told Trish, "Greg wants us to do a marriage conference for his church in October." Trisha's vision for creating something beyond sharing our testimony on Sunday mornings was coming into fruition. I texted him back, "We're in. We'd love to do that."

We worked each week to create content for the marriage conference, and the six sessions we developed became the foundation of the book we wrote two years later.

After that first conference, in October of 2010, God began to provide opportunities, in ways we couldn't imagine, to travel across the country and share our marriage conference. In 2014, we received a speaking request for a church in New Hampshire. The pastor and I connected and worked out the details of the weekend. We were to do two sessions on Friday night, three on Saturday morning, and then speak at both of their Sunday-morning church services.

About a week before the conference in New Hampshire, I posted on Facebook how excited we were to do our RefineUs Marriage Conference there. A few minutes later, a friend texted, asking if I could talk for a few minutes. He and his wife were longtime friends of ours, and he had recently attended a church leadership conference where Trish and I shared our testimony.

He said, "I saw you are going to New Hampshire. You know, I lived there for thirteen years. It is an amazing place with amazing people, but you may be a little much for some people there."

I said, "What do you mean, 'a little much'?"

He said, "The people of New England aren't as open and vulnerable as you and Trish. You primarily speak at churches in the Midwest and the South of the US. The Northeast is different. I want to prepare you; even if people look mad while you speak, they could love what you are saying."

We arrived at the church and met the pastor. He was incredibly gracious and gave us a tour of the church, set us up with audio and video, did a mic check, and then went back to his office. He said, "I want to prepare you guys that your story is very open and vulnerable. It resonates with me deeply, and it's part of the reason I brought you in this weekend. But culturally, vulnerability isn't something people in the Northeast are known for."

Trish and I talked through our outline for the conference's first session, and she asked me if I would adjust any content considering what the pastor had told us. I said, "I don't plan on it. I don't want to offend anyone, but I also want to be faithful to the message we are called to share." So, we decided to move forward as planned.

The first session of our conference was about God's vision for marriage. In the middle of that session, I shared my choice in 2005 to have an affair with Trish's best friend. As I confessed this part of our story, a few couples got up and started walking toward the back of the room. I didn't think much of it at the time, but then a few minutes later, more couples got up and left. Over the next ten minutes, we estimated that at least ten couples had left the conference thirty minutes into our first session.

We closed that session in prayer, then went back into the pastor's office. I was feeling very self-conscious. Our second session was just a few minutes away and was significantly more intense than the first, as I would talk about being sexually abused as a kid and struggling with pornography for the first ten years of marriage.

When I get nervous, I sweat like crazy. I don't have hair, so there's nothing to stop sweat from streaming down my face. I was soaked with sweat trying to figure out what to do. Finally, I told Trish, "If we don't share this truth, then we are compromising God's call on our hearts. I'll be sensitive in sharing during this session, but we should move forward."

We got back onstage and shared the content from our hearts, and by God's grace, no one got up and left. But we still had three sessions to teach the next day. We wondered if anyone would come back. To our surprise, everyone who attended the first two sessions returned on Saturday.

As we walked off the stage after the final session, a man in tears approached and asked if he could talk to me. So, I guided him to an area in the auditorium where we could have more privacy.

The man said, "I can't thank you enough for this weekend. God brought you here to set me free. I'm eighty-four years old, and I've been married for sixty-four years. I was sexually abused when I was ten, and I've lived in shame and guilt for the last seventy-four years. God brought you here to set me free from that shame."

I was speechless. Then eventually I said, "Can I give you a hug?" He agreed, and we embraced. He hugged me like a ten-year-old boy hugs his dad.

He continued, "I've never told anyone about this until last night. After your second session, during the discussion time, I told my wife about the abuse. It felt like a weight was lifted from me."

Tears started pouring down my face; it was all I could do not to break out into weeping. I had seen this gentleman throughout the weekend. His arms were often crossed. His demeanor appeared bothered at worst and uninterested at best. What I had interpreted as disapproval was his seventy-four-year battle with the disapproval of himself. I had grossly misunderstood the moment.

We embraced again, and I shared with him some steps I'd taken to overcome the shame of my abuse and the guilt of my porn addiction. I prayed for him, and then in a divine moment, he asked if he could pray for me. I don't remember the totality of his prayer, but I recall him praying, "Heavenly Father, remind Justin that You are using his words to uncover and deconstruct shame."

I'll never forget that moment. That prayer represents my hope for this chapter. I pray God will use my words to disarm the power and grip shame has on your life, so you can move from trying to be perfect to being real.

Before we talk about overcoming shame, we first need to define it, identify it, and discover how we accumulate it.

defining shame

First, let's define shame. *Merriam-Webster's Dictionary* defines the word as "a painful emotion caused by the consciousness of guilt, shortcoming, or impropriety."[1] That is the literary definition of shame. But there is also a spiritual definition of shame. Spiritually speaking, shame goes beyond what we've done to the very core of who we are. When I think about guilt, I see it as transactional. I do something wrong and feel bad for it. Guilt is based on choices and behavior. It can be overcome with an apology or an ask for forgiveness.

Shame goes beyond the transaction of emotion for what I've done wrong and seeps into the soul of who I am. Shame doesn't cause me to feel like what I've done is terrible; it convinces me that I am horrible because I've done something wrong. Shame allows me to know the freedom of forgiveness, without allowing me to feel free, even though I know I'm forgiven. Shame goes to the core of who I am and how I see God.

In his book *Shame and Grace*, Lewis Smedes gave this definition of shame: "The difference between guilt and shame is very clear—in theory. We feel guilty for what we do. We feel shame for what we are. A person feels guilt because he *did* something wrong. A person feels shame because he *is* something wrong."[2]

Guilt is a momentary spiritual transaction. Shame is a long-standing spiritual condition. There is an epidemic of shame in the hearts and souls of Jesus' followers today. We feel shame in our friendships, in our marriages, as parents, as children, as employees, as employers. We accumulate guilt over time, and because we've been conditioned to be perfect and not real, that unacknowledged and unconfessed guilt becomes a part of us.

Smedes gave examples of the feeling of shame and how to identify the shame you may be unknowingly living with:

> I sometimes feel as if I am a fake.
>
> I feel that if people who admire me really knew me they might have contempt for me.
>
> I feel inadequate; I seldom feel as if I am up to what is expected of me.
>
> When I look inside myself, I seldom feel any joy at what I am.
>
> I feel inferior to the really good people I know.
>
> I feel as if God must be disgusted with me.
>
> I feel flawed inside, blemished somehow, dirty sometimes.
>
> I feel as if I just cannot measure up to what I ought to be.
>
> I feel as if I will never be acceptable.[3]

the places we find shame

Finding out, at age thirty-six, that my dad wasn't my biological father caused a lot of the emotions and insecurities I had felt during childhood to make sense. But growing up, I didn't have that knowledge. I was only aware that I was a disappointment to my dad.

I am the oldest of four siblings. I have a sister and two brothers. My dad graduated from high school and went straight into the workforce. He was a mechanic and worked on cars when I was young. As I got older, he became a machinist and started working in factories, reading blueprints and making parts based on the drawings he was given.

My mind doesn't work that way. I am the least mechanical person alive. But I wanted so badly to be with my dad that I often tried to work on the car with him in the garage. I handed him tools much like a nurse gives a surgeon instruments. The problem was that I didn't know the difference between a socket and a crescent wrench. I couldn't distinguish between a Phillips-head screwdriver and an Allen wrench. So rather than bonding, working with my dad in the garage was disappointing. My time with him usually ended with him saying, "Just go in the house with your mom."

My dad loved fishing and hunting. To his credit, he tried multiple times to get me to love them too. Unfortunately, fishing involves two things I struggle with: being outside exposed to mosquitoes and silently watching a bobber on the water's surface, waiting for a bite. Usually, the only thing that got bit was me, and I was miserable.

He tried to take me hunting too, but that required waking up early. I was not interested in getting up at four in the morning to freeze my butt off in a tree stand. Hunting, like fishing, involved silence. You had to be quiet, and that was a problem for me. I get bored quickly. For a few years when I became a teenager, my dad invited me to go deer hunting with him, but he could tell I hated it, so eventually, he stopped asking.

I know my dad was proud of me for my sports accomplishments, and he was proud of the husband and father I eventually became, but I grew up feeling ashamed that I wasn't the son he truly wanted. I thought if I could be more of a craftsman, learn to ride a Harley-Davidson, and tolerate going fishing, he might be prouder of me.

parents

For some, our parents are the first source of our shame. Our relationship with our parents informs how we process wounds and guilt that eventually become shame. Maybe, like me, you've never felt accepted for who you are by your parents. Perhaps you still feel that way. Maybe your parents were a source of shame through the things they said:

- "You should be ashamed of yourself."
- "Why can't you be more like your brother/sister?"
- "You are such an idiot."
- "You are disgusting."
- "When are you going to make something of yourself?"
- "Keep acting like that, and you'll never get anyone to love you."

To give away our shame, we have to disconnect what people have said about us from who we are. I've learned that those who project shame onto others usually have unresolved shame themselves. That is why this is so important. To end the cycle of shame, you have to identify its source and disconnect your shame from who you are.

ourselves

In some cases, we are the source of our shame. How we deal with sin can produce shame in our hearts. We can create shame from the sins we commit and the sins committed against us.

For about a year after the affair, I lived in shame. Not a day went by that I didn't think about all the damage I had caused, all the hurt I had inflicted, and all the relationships I had damaged. I knew in my head that Trisha forgave me, but my heart couldn't accept it.

Our marriage, in many ways, was in recovery mode, and we were growing in our love for each other. But the daily pain of my decisions ate away at my heart. It affected my view of myself. It affected my relationship with my kids and with God. I felt unworthy and undeserving of love.

I remember standing in the kitchen and breaking down in tears, feeling the weight of my shame. Finally, Trisha said, "Grace is only grace if you accept it. I've worked hard to extend it, but you aren't accepting it. I forgive you. I think it is time you forgive yourself." Those words were like water to my thirsty soul. Before that moment, I didn't think I could ever forgive myself.

Maybe you know all about God's grace, but you haven't allowed it to penetrate your heart. Instead, you find your identity in your mistakes. Shame is a badge you wear to punish yourself for the mistakes you've made, the regrets you've accumulated. You ask yourself:

- If I forgive myself, doesn't that mean I'm getting away with something?
- If I forgive myself, doesn't that make it seem like I'm not paying for what I've done?
- If I forgive myself, who will remind me how much of a screwup I am?

Shame for your sins says, "You don't deserve forgiveness."

Maybe your shame isn't over the sins you've committed; it originates with sins committed against you. If shame for your sins says, "You don't deserve forgiveness," shame for the sins of others says, "You deserved what happened to you."

Maybe you were physically or emotionally abused when you were a kid, and you convinced yourself that the abuse was your fault and you deserved it. Maybe you were sexually abused as a child, and you told someone, but they didn't believe you; or they believed you but didn't do anything about it. Maybe you were sexually assaulted in college, and you carry shame because you think you shouldn't have been at that party, gone on that date, or put yourself in that situation. You think the assault was your fault. Maybe your spouse cheated on you, your parent abandoned you, or your friend betrayed you. Shame says, "You deserved what happened to you."

Lewis Smedes said, "We deceive ourselves with the falsehood that we are unworthy human beings. We support our deception with the plausible reasons why we should feel unworthy."[4]

Being honest with ourselves about our shame is a necessary step in overcoming it.

religion

The final source of shame is religion. I don't have experience in other expressions of religion other than the evangelical church. I wish the American Church wasn't such a huge source of shame, but for many, that is the case.

One of my first experiences with religious shame came when I was twelve or thirteen. We were in a congregational church meeting. I don't remember whether the church was voting on the budget or hiring a staff member, but I recall a woman toward the back of the sanctuary offering a dissenting opinion on the proposal. She continued pushing back, until the man leading the meeting mentioned her recent divorce and questioned publicly if she was still qualified to be a voting member of the church. The room went silent; the woman got up and left.

While not always public, the people of Jesus have often made others feel the shame that Jesus died to overcome. Romans 8:1–2 says, "Therefore, there is now no condemnation for those who are in Christ Jesus, because through Christ Jesus the law of the Spirit who gives life has set you free from the law of sin and death."

The word *condemnation* in Greek means "judgment" or "to find guilty." In a 2017 survey, Lifeway Research asked 2,002 people between the ages of 23 and 30 why they left the evangelical church. Thirty-two percent of them said, "Church members seem judgmental."[5]

> Being honest with ourselves about our shame is a necessary step in overcoming it.

In Christ there is no judgment, but in Christ followers, there is condemnation. This is nothing new. Religion has been causing shame since the time of Jesus.

Luke 15 is one of my favorite chapters in the entire Bible. In it, Jesus shared three parables to combat the condemnation and shame the religious leaders projected onto tax collectors and sinners.

> Now the tax collectors and sinners were all gathering
> around to hear Jesus. But the Pharisees and the teachers
> of the law muttered, "This man welcomes sinners and
> eats with them." (Luke 15:1–2).

Jesus then told the three parables about things lost and found. The first two parables describe someone losing a valuable object and turning over heaven and earth to find it. The third parable tells of two sons—one who knows he's lost and one who doesn't. But the father's heart for both demonstrates God's love for us in the midst of our shame.

> Jesus continued: "There was a man who had two sons. The
> younger one said to his father, 'Father, give me my share of
> the estate.' So he divided his property between them.
>
> "Not long after that, the younger son got together all
> he had, set off for a distant country and there squandered
> his wealth in wild living. After he had spent everything,
> there was a severe famine in that whole country, and he
> began to be in need. So he went and hired himself out to
> a citizen of that country, who sent him to his fields to feed
> pigs. He longed to fill his stomach with the pods that the
> pigs were eating, but no one gave him anything.
>
> "When he came to his senses, he said, 'How many
> of my father's hired servants have food to spare, and
> here I am starving to death! I will set out and go back to
> my father and say to him: Father, I have sinned against
> heaven and against you. I am no longer worthy to be

called your son; make me like one of your hired servants.'
So he got up and went to his father.

"But while he was still a long way off, his father saw
him and was filled with compassion for him; he ran to his
son, threw his arms around him and kissed him.

"The son said to him, 'Father, I have sinned against
heaven and against you. I am no longer worthy to be
called your son.'

"But the father said to his servants, 'Quick! Bring the
best robe and put it on him. Put a ring on his finger and
sandals on his feet. Bring the fattened calf and kill it. Let's
have a feast and celebrate. For this son of mine was dead
and is alive again; he was lost and is found.' So they began
to celebrate." (Luke 15:11–24)

Jesus told a story about a son who chose to leave home and live in a distant country. This son thought that his life would be better on his own, away
from his father. He didn't want his father's rules and restrictions, so he said
to his father, in so many words, "I know you aren't dead, but I want to live
my life as if you are. Give me what is mine now; I don't want to wait until you
die." Graciously, his father conceded and gave his younger son his share of the
inheritance. The son went to a distant land and almost immediately began to
process the shame of his choices. I want to look at three ways this younger son
processed shame, and perhaps we'll discover ourselves in the story.

three destructive ways to deal with shame

There are three ways we try to deal with shame that do more harm than
good.

medicate it

The first way we deal with shame is to medicate it. When we feel the shame of our choices or choices made against us, we want the pain of those choices to go away. Instead of dealing with the reality of our shame, we try to numb our hurt.

> Not long after that, the younger son got together all he had, set off for a distant country and there squandered his wealth in wild living. (Luke 15:13)

When you are in the distant country of shame, you may not squander your wealth on wild living, but:

- You may drown your abuse in excessive drinking.
- You may view pornography to satisfy your loneliness.
- You may escape the pain of a relationship by binge-watching Netflix.
- You may look to food to take away the pain of abandonment.
- You may give yourself to person after person to fulfill your desire to be loved.

When we deal with sin (ours or others') by pursuing more sin, it doesn't break the cycle of shame; it perpetuates it. We may find momentary relief from our shame by "squandering our wealth on wild living," but we don't leave the distant country and return to the Father.

meditate on it

The second way we deal with shame is to meditate on it.

> After he had spent everything, there was a severe famine
> in that whole country, and he began to be in need. So he
> went and hired himself out to a citizen of that country,
> who sent him to his fields to feed pigs. He longed to fill his
> stomach with the pods that the pigs were eating, but no
> one gave him anything.
>
> When he came to his senses, he said, "How many of
> my father's hired servants have food to spare, and here I
> am starving to death!" (Luke 15:14–17)

This is the self-talk that shame teaches us to master. *You are not worthy. You are not loved. You are not valued. You'll never amount to anything. You'll always struggle with this. You'll always be single. You'll never be a good parent. You'll always be in debt. You'll never be free from this addiction. You'll always be a cheater. You can't be forgiven.*

This beloved son, who squandered everything his father gave him, meditated on how unworthy he was. He went from having servants to being a servant. He went from feast to famine. He went from having plenty to wanting to eat with pigs. He meditated on all he had lost, all he didn't have, all he didn't deserve.

make up for it

When you meditate on shame long enough, you eventually move into the final way we deal with shame: we try to make up for it.

> "I will set out and go back to my father and say to him:
> Father, I have sinned against heaven and against you. I

am no longer worthy to be called your son; make me like one of your hired servants." So he got up and went to his father. (Luke 15:18–20)

After experiencing the pain of his shame, this son wanted to go home, but he no longer believed he could be received as a son. So, he decided to offer himself as a servant. As a hired servant, he might be able to pay his father back. He might be able to redeem himself and perform his way into his father's good graces again.

Maybe for you, that is the lie that shame has convinced you to believe: You've made so many mistakes that you will have to earn your way back. You will have to prove your love to God. You will have to perform well to get God to love you again.

A few months after the affair, a good friend and mentor asked me if we could have coffee. At Starbucks, I recounted for him my sinful choices, our separation, our counseling journey, and how, just a few weeks earlier, I'd gone back home. He was deeply moved and very supportive and gracious. I said, "Mark, all I want to do is spend the rest of my life making it up to her."

He said, "JD, that's not how grace works. You can never make it up to her. That's what's so amazing about grace. She forgives despite you not being able to make it up to her."

Shame will tell you that just a little more *good* will outweigh your *bad*. Shame will convince you that if you try a little harder, you can finally be the husband you promised you'd be. Shame will say to you that if you act better, you can make up for all your mess-ups.

But living in shame diminishes God's grace and keeps you from God's best. Here is what happened when the son returned home:

But while he was still a long way off, his father saw him and was filled with compassion for him; he ran to his son, threw his arms around him and kissed him.

The son said to him, "Father, I have sinned against heaven and against you. I am no longer worthy to be called your son."

But the father said to his servants, "Quick! Bring the best robe and put it on him. Put a ring on his finger and sandals on his feet. Bring the fattened calf and kill it. Let's have a feast and celebrate." (Luke 15:20–23)

While the son was still a long way off, the father ran toward him. Your proximity to God doesn't determine His commitment to run to you. You can be a long way off; He will come running. Remember how when Adam and Eve sinned, shame caused them to hide from God? Then what happened? God went searching for them (Gen. 3). Our sin and shame don't intimidate God. If you decide to come home, He will come running.

how to give away your shame

How do we give away our shame? What is the practical process of returning to the Father? Here are a few principles. They are not an equation to work out, but more of a process to work through.

Often, we confuse forgiveness of sin with healing from sin. When we confess our sins, God is faithful and just and forgives us, as far as the east is from the west. But healing from sin is a process that can take time.

identify what's hurt you

The first step is to identify what's hurt you. For some, this is what counselors call "Big T" trauma, such as abuse, neglect, divorce, or betrayal. For others, this could be "little t" trauma that has accumulated or has a pattern in your life. For still others, there may be a specific sin you've committed that has hurt you and your relationship with God. You've tried to avoid it and hoped it would go away.

deal with your regrets

Second, you have to deal with your regrets. What do you do with your regret? Scripture has one word that will overcome your regrets: repentance. Repentance is the pathway to overcoming regret.

Repentance is a big word, but all it means is "a sincere sorrow for wrongdoing" and "to turn in the opposite direction." Paul talked about this in a letter to the Corinthians.

To give you some background, the church in Corinth was a mess. Paul had sent them one letter, in which he went after them. We don't know the content of that letter, but he must have taken off the gloves, because he confessed it was harsh, direct, and hurt the readers. So, that is the context for his comments in the next letter.

> Even if I caused you sorrow by my letter, I do not regret it. Though I did regret it—I see that my letter hurt you, but only for a little while—yet now I am happy, not because you were made sorry, but because your sorrow led you to repentance. For you became sorrowful as God intended and so were not harmed in any way by us. Godly sorrow brings repentance that leads to salvation and leaves no regret, but worldly sorrow brings death. (2 Cor. 7:8–10)

Godly sorrow is conviction and leaves no regrets. Worldly sorrow is shame and brings death. Dealing with our regrets begins by recognizing them.

One of the parenting principles we taught our kids is that it's better to confess than be caught. You lose more trust if you are caught than if you confess. But if you are a parent, you know that confession happens way less than being caught.

> Repentance is the pathway
> to overcoming regret.

I think God wants us to come to Him in the same way. The first step in repentance is recognition—not being sorry for being caught, but being sorry for what we've done. When our kids apologize to us, the first question we ask is "What are you sorry for?" It's an opportunity for them to say whether they are sorry for what they did or for getting caught. We can't overcome our regrets until we acknowledge them.

Back to the story of the Prodigal Son. On his way home, he prepared a speech for his dad. He would tell his father he had sinned against both heaven and his father and that he was no longer worthy of being called a son. He had so many regrets, but he was repentant.

As soon as his father saw him, he ran and embraced his son—the one who had been homeless and feeding pigs. He embraced his son who had squandered all his money on wild living. He embraced his son who wanted to live as if his father were dead. All of that was in the past. His son had returned home from the distant country.

When the son started into his prepared speech, the father interrupted him. He didn't want to hear what shame had helped write. He cut off the speech and ordered the best robe to be put on his son—one that would give him dignity. He asked for a ring to be put on his son's finger, because that reflected his identity. He was not a slave, but a son. The father told his servants to put sandals on his son's feet, because that showed his value. Servants were barefoot, not sons.

God does the same thing for you. No matter how long you've been living in the distant country of shame. Your Father invites you to come home. He is waiting. He doesn't want you make up for your mistakes or mess-ups. He doesn't ask you to redeem yourself. You can't. That is what Jesus did on the cross.

He will trade your shame for forgiveness. He will trade your guilt for His grace. He will trade your hiding for His presence. Give away your shame so you can rediscover your identity.

chapter 8

rediscover your identity

your self-worth isn't based on how you feel but on what God says

> "Most people spend a lifetime trying to become what they already are."
>
> Neil Anderson, *Living Free in Christ*

Two of my four sons earned college basketball scholarships. My oldest son, Micah, was a good player and had a little college interest. He is 6'1", although he'll tell you he's 6'2". He had a few small offers come in, but when he got an offer from the top NAIA (National Association of Intercollegiate Athletics) basketball team in the country, Indiana Wesleyan University, it was a gift we didn't expect. During our earlier visit to Indiana Wesleyan, Micah hadn't played well in the open gyms and was discouraged and convinced he wouldn't receive an offer. When the head coach offered Micah a scholarship, I thought Micah was going to commit on the spot. He did commit a few days later.

My son Isaiah is 6'9" and was ranked in the top twenty players in his class in Indiana by the *Indianapolis Star* newspaper. From the end of his sophomore year of high school, we recognized that his recruitment would be different from Micah's. However, we weren't prepared for how brutal the recruiting journey would be.

The pressure to perform as a sixteen- or seventeen-year-old athlete can be overwhelming. Every move is evaluated. Writers watch a portion of a game and write an entire article on a player's strengths and weaknesses. What they write can determine coaches' interest levels.

The summer before Isaiah's junior year of high school was in 2020, which you may remember as the summer of Covid-19. The Indiana AAU (Amateur Athletic Union) basketball season looked different. There were just four weekend tournaments, and parents were the only spectators permitted in the gym. No coaches were allowed on-site. Instead, games were streamed online, and coaches watched and evaluated remotely. Isaiah had some good moments but nothing remarkable.

When Micah was in high school, he played for an AAU team called the Tennessee Tigers. Their coach, Chip Smith, advocated for Micah and helped secure his scholarship to Indiana Wesleyan. After the Indiana AAU season, I saw on Twitter that the Tennessee Tigers were playing in a tournament in Atlanta. So, I texted Chip and let him know that if he needed a 6'9" power forward for the upcoming tournament, we'd fly Isaiah down to meet the team. Almost immediately, he texted and said he had a jersey for Isaiah.

Isaiah arrived in Atlanta a few hours before the first game. Chip and the team had driven down to Atlanta from Nashville, so we paid for an Uber to take Isaiah to the gym. He met the players, put on his uniform, and Chip drew out a few plays for him on the clipboard. His first play in the first game was a steal and breakaway dunk on a fast break.

That play set the tone for the next three days. Isaiah played incredibly, and his phone started to blow up with coaches calling. Division 1, Division 2, and NAIA coaches began texting, calling, and visiting Isaiah. Finally, two days after the tournament in Atlanta, Isaiah received his first full-ride scholarship offer.

The next few months were a blur. We went on eleven college visits, and Isaiah received an offer on or before every visit. As a parent, it was incredible. But as the exposure increased and the offers piled up, so did the pressure for Isaiah to produce.

Finally, the summer before his senior year of high school, he was on a highly talented AAU team that played a demanding national schedule. Isaiah was coming off knee surgery and had a few colleges on his list from which he wanted to receive offers. They texted before the tournament in Dallas to let him know they'd be at the games. They were looking forward to seeing him play. He didn't play badly in Dallas, but he needed to impress them more to receive the offers. This pattern repeated itself each weekend of the summer.

The coaching staff from Huntington University, a small NAIA university in northern Indiana, came to everything. They came to watch Isaiah practice. They showed up at workouts. They called and texted and spent time getting to know him. Then, when Isaiah had his surgery and wasn't yet cleared to play, they came to watch him sit on the bench in street clothes. Their expectations weren't determined by his ability to perform or produce. Instead, they were interested in him.

A few weeks before Isaiah's senior year, he committed to Huntington University. He knew that they wanted him as a person as much as a player. The school and the coaching staff felt like a fit.

Isaiah moved to Huntington, and a short time later, the team started open gyms. They played a few times a week, and Isaiah's play was inconsistent at best. He wasn't feeling comfortable. He'd call or text me after each workout or open gym:

- "Didn't shoot well. It was embarrassing."

- "I'm hesitating before every shot. I'm shooting not to miss instead of to score."
- "Don't feel comfortable with my shot. I'm not myself."
- "I'm in my head."

After about a week of this, my wife and I FaceTimed Isaiah. We had a long conversation about the recruiting process and his mission to impress every time he stepped on the floor the previous year. He was playing from a place of wanting to be wanted. He was playing to be accepted. He was playing to try to earn approval and love.

But now, he is in a place that loves him. He is with people who want him. He is accepted. He is wanted. He is the highest-ranked recruit this coaching staff has secured. He doesn't have to play to be approved. He can play from a place of approval. He can play from a place of belonging. He can play from a place of security.

Just because we can doesn't always mean we do.

After one of the first games of the year, Coach Alford approached me in the hallway outside of the locker room and said, "Isaiah is just not himself. We love and believe in him, but he is trying hard to prove himself. He doesn't have to prove himself. He's already proved himself; that is why he is here."

Isaiah and I talked after the game, and I wanted to get beyond how he was playing and try to understand what he was feeling. I said, "Isaiah, all the coaches believe in you. You have a role on the team, and they have a vision for your career here. What are you feeling?"

He said, "I just feel that I am letting them down with every shot I miss and every time I mess up on defense."

I said, "Isaiah, you are still playing to impress them. You are still trying to prove yourself. You are trying to earn their approval. But you are already approved. You are already accepted. You are already invited in. You don't have to prove anything. Your worth isn't tied to your performance. You are worthy."

For the previous two years, his self-esteem had been based on his performance. The better he performed, the more valuable he felt. The more valuable he felt, the higher his self-esteem. Failing to live up to his expectations triggered an essential process of finding his identity outside of his performance on the court. His performance determined his self-esteem, and his self-esteem informed his self-worth.

self-esteem vs. self-worth

For many of us, our self-esteem is determined by our performance. And we believe the lie that our self-esteem determines our self-worth. *Cambridge Dictionary* defines *self-esteem* as "confidence in one's own worth or abilities."[1] How we perceive ourselves is directly connected to how worthy or valuable we feel.

I love how author Kendra Cherry described self-esteem: "Self-esteem is your subjective sense of your overall worth or value."[2] The key word in this definition is *subjective*. Subjective means biased. It's how we perceive ourselves. How we perceive ourselves isn't always accurate. A quick search on Amazon for "books on self-esteem"—and the over forty thousand titles it returns—demonstrates we have a self-esteem deficit. We continue to try to find self-worth by improving our self-esteem.

There is a vast difference between your self-esteem and your self-worth. Self-esteem is conditional—it factors in your wounds. Self-esteem is your perception of yourself. It gathers all your hurt and rejection, and all the lies you believe about yourself, and allows you to rehearse those things in your mind. Self-esteem remembers the one insult you received last week and forgets the ten compliments. Self-esteem is an emotional roller coaster that leaves you never looking good enough, never being smart enough, never achieving enough, never accumulating enough.

Self-worth isn't close to self-esteem. Your self-worth is God-given. Your self-worth is nonnegotiable. Your self-worth is based not on who you are but on who God is. Your self-worth can't be taken away; it can't be degraded; it can't be robbed. Your self-worth was given to you before the creation of the world. Your attractiveness, beauty, weight, complexion, hair color, smile, body shape, tax bracket, employment status, marital status, and past mistakes and failures have nothing to do with your self-worth. You are valuable for the single reason that God created you in His image.

Confusing our self-esteem with self-worth is an indication we have an identity crisis. Self-esteem originates in how we feel about ourselves, and self-worth begins in what God says about us. Finding our identity in our self-esteem and not our self-worth sets us on a path of inauthenticity, hiding, and pretending.

finding your identity apart from God

Every human has bought into the lie that we can find our identity in something other than what God says about us. Unfortunately, this pattern didn't start with us; we've been broken in this area for a long time.

> The serpent was the shrewdest of all the wild animals the LORD God had made. One day he asked the woman, "Did God really say you must not eat the fruit from any of the trees in the garden?"

"Of course we may eat fruit from the trees in the
garden," the woman replied. "It's only the fruit from the
tree in the middle of the garden that we are not allowed
to eat. God said, 'You must not eat it or even touch it; if
you do, you will die.'"

"You won't die!" the serpent replied to the woman.
"God knows that your eyes will be opened as soon as you
eat it, and you will be like God, knowing both good and evil."

The woman was convinced. She saw that the tree
was beautiful and its fruit looked delicious, and she
wanted the wisdom it would give her. So she took some of
the fruit and ate it. Then she gave some to her husband,
who was with her, and he ate it, too. At that moment their
eyes were opened, and they suddenly felt shame at their
nakedness. So they sewed fig leaves together to cover
themselves. (Gen. 3:1–7 NLT)

Initially, the serpent didn't tell Eve anything. He simply asked a question, "Did God really say you must not eat the fruit from any of the trees in
the garden?" To tempt Eve, Satan used part of the truth of what God said,
twisted with a distortion of the truth.

When we start to doubt God's character, we begin to question God's
ways. That is what happened with Eve. "The woman was convinced" that
God was holding out on her. God wasn't enough. She believed this lie that she
could find truth, know good and evil, and be like God. She thought she could
have an identity outside of what God told her, that she could create her own
identity separate from God.

> Self-esteem originates in
> how we feel about ourselves,
> and self-worth begins in
> what God says about us.

In his book *Winning the War in Your Mind*, pastor Craig Groeschel said, "A lie believed as truth will affect your life as if it were true."[3]

On January 13, 2018, in Hawaii, fear of an impending ballistic missile attack caused thirty-eight minutes of panic. The *New York Times* published this description of the military drill that two dispatch workers confused as real:

> An early-morning emergency alert mistakenly warning of
> an incoming ballistic missile attack was dispatched to cell-
> phones across Hawaii on Saturday, setting off widespread
> panic in a state that was already on edge because of escalat-
> ing tensions between the United States and North Korea.[4]

The missile attack wasn't real, but the panic generated by the false report was very real. A lie believed as though it were true carries the power of truth in our lives. So many of us have bought into the lie that we can find identity and self-worth in something or someone other than God. This belief has the power to keep us from becoming who God says we are.

There are an unlimited number of places we go to try to find identity when we believe this lie, but a few of them I think are universal to most of us as we journey with Jesus.

outward appearance

The lie with outward appearance is "Who you are is how you look." Our culture is preoccupied with physical beauty, wealth, attractiveness, and all that is easily visible. So many have bought into the lie that says our identity and value are in direct relationship to our physical attractiveness. The result is that people are consumed with outward appearance.

Maybe you are saying, "Justin, isn't *consumed* a pretty strong word?" In 2021, Americans spent $49.2 billion dollars on cosmetics.[5] Although this hasn't been a need of mine for several years, Americans spent $15 billion on hair-care products in 2017.[6] The dieting industry in America is one of the most robust in the entire world. Over 45 million Americans put themselves on diets each year, and we spend $33 billion on diet food.[7] We aren't even touching the money spent on gym memberships, cosmetic surgery, or diet supplements. We have bought into the lie that looking a certain way, being a little skinnier, having a clearer complexion, appearing slightly more attractive will make us *enough*. We'll be admired, respected, accepted, loved.

The truth is that the body is the temple of the Holy Spirit. We should steward and care for our bodies and maintain healthy eating and exercise habits. We distort that truth when we believe the lie that who I am is how I look.

academic or athletic achievement

The base of the achievement lie is "Who you are is what you accomplish." I got cut from the basketball team in seventh and eighth grades. I told myself after that experience that I never wanted anyone to tell me again that I wasn't good enough. I worked hard and made the freshman basketball team. My sophomore year, I dressed and played on the varsity team. At our basketball banquet in March, I received a varsity letter.

Because my family didn't have a lot of money, we couldn't afford to buy a letterman jacket, so we put one on layaway. For those too young to remember, layaway involved setting up a payment plan with the store for a large purchase. By the time we paid off my letterman jacket, it was July. I wasn't deterred by the 95 degree weather. I put on my letterman jacket, jumped on my moped, and drove around our small town, flaunting my athletic accomplishment.

Many of us are conditioned from a young age that our grades will define us. Our success in the classroom is paramount to our success in the world. The grades you earned, the classes you took, the college you chose—all these things served to define the success you might attain and acquire. Maybe approval from your parents was dependent on the grades you brought home. Maybe you come from a line of academic overachievers, and you've always felt pressure to perform.

Maybe your identity was wrapped up in your athletic success. Your parents constantly compared your talents and ability to that of other teammates or an older sibling. Your mom loved soccer, so you felt pressure to love soccer. Your dad was an all-state quarterback, so you thought you had to live up to his accomplishments. Your identity became grounded in what you accomplished or didn't accomplish on the field or court.

We are more than the sum of our academic or athletic achievements. When we believe the lie "Who you are is what you accomplish," we diminish the identity that God has placed in each of us that goes beyond our accomplishments and achievements.

vocational performance

The vocational-performance lie finds power in convincing us that "Who you are is what you do." Several studies have been done exploring the mortality

rate in men after retirement. In an article on WebMD titled "Early Retirement, Early Death?," medical writer Daniel DeNoon cited a study among
Shell Oil employees that showed people who retire at age 55 and live to be at
least 65 generally die sooner than people who retire at 65. He wrote, "People
who retire at 55 are 89% more likely to die in the 10 years after retirement
than those who retire at 65."[8]

It seems there is a direct connection between finding your identity
through work and your ability to adapt to life after retirement.[9]

From an early age, we are asked one question more than any other:
"What do you want to be when you grow up?" This isn't a question about your
gifts, passion, or even God's call on your life. This is a question about vocation. What is toxic about the question is the word *be*. The way we phrase the
question suggests that what we do for a living when we grow up is the same
thing as who we are when we grow up. For many of us, we are what we do.

When Trisha and I were separated in 2005, I realized I had bought into
this lie, "Who you are is what you do." I was a pastor, and for the first ten
years of our marriage, that is where I found my identity. I didn't realize how
destructive this lie had become until one afternoon sitting in a porch swing
with my three boys.

During our separation, I was staying with longtime family friends, and
Trish and I had worked out a mutual arrangement for me to spend time with
our boys. One afternoon, we were sitting on the front porch of the Wilhems'
house, and Micah, who was nine at the time, asked me if Trish and I were
going to get a divorce. I said, "I am not sure if we will get divorced, but I do
know that I am not going to be the pastor of Genesis Church anymore."

Micah immediately panicked. He stood up, started crying, and said,
"You have to be the pastor! I'm the pastor's son! You have to be the pastor!
I'm the pastor's son!"

The other two boys, not realizing the implications of Micah's words, but relating to how upset he was, began to cry too. I grabbed Micah and pulled him close. "I'm sorry, buddy. I'm really sorry," I said.

"Dad, you have to be the pastor. I'm the pastor's son," he said, as he buried his head in my chest.

That was a defining moment for me. I realized that not only had I constructed my own identity around what I did; our entire family found their identity, not in Jesus, but in my pastoral position.

We don't ask, "Who do you want to be when you grow up?" We ask, "What do you want to be when you grow up?" When we reduce our answer to a vocation, we buy into the lie "Who you are is what you do."

social media influence

This is something we don't readily admit, but when we find our identity in social media, the lie we believe is "Who you are is how much influence you have." We measure our identity by our likes and comments. I am not coming down on social media, as I have active Twitter, Facebook, and Instagram accounts, but it's easy to find our value in what pictures other people like and how many times our IG Story is viewed.

Pastor Shawn Johnson said this in *Attacking Anxiety*:

> The next time you spend some time scrolling, take inventory of two things:
> The types of posts you see
> The way it makes you feel
> I can almost guarantee what the answer is going to be to both of those. The answer to the first question is, you are going to see everyone's highlight reel. Very few

people ever decide to post the low points of their lives. Which means, if you are anything like me, the answer to the second question is, it'll make you feel like you aren't enough. Here are the thoughts that run through my head: Wow, I don't have that great of a car, house, family, or vacation. I guess I'm not that great of a parent. Or friend. Or employee. Or leader. I guess I don't really do anything all that important. I guess I don't have a purpose like they do. I don't travel like she does. I don't earn an income like him. I don't walk and talk like they do. Maybe I'm just less than. It's almost impossible to spend a significant amount of time on social media and not feel more insecure and unstable.[10]

I don't get off social media and feel like I have it all together. I get off social media wondering why more people didn't like my post, why I had only two comments, and why more people didn't view my Instagram Story.

family tree

The lie of the family tree tells you, "Who you are is who you are related to." Maybe you find your identity in being "Sarah's mom" or "Ben's dad." Your kids get all your focus and attention. They get prioritized over your marriage and your relationship with God. Your life revolves around your kids' needs, and you find your identity in being a parent.

Maybe you grew up in the shadow of an older brother or sister. They got all the breaks and attention. They won all the awards. They were the favorite of your parents, teachers, and relatives. Your identity was shaped by not measuring up to their standard.

Maybe your identity is in your marital status. You are single, and your life has been reduced to feeling incomplete because you aren't married. You've been on all the blind dates, tried all the apps, swiped right and left, and you are still alone. Every holiday is a reminder that you haven't found "the one" yet.

Many people have a hard time feeling close to God as heavenly Father because they don't have a healthy relationship with their earthly father. Their earthly father left or abused them, and they can't relate to God in an intimate way, because their relationship with their dad is so complicated.

Earlier I mentioned my journey after finding out the man I thought of as father wasn't my biological father. It was earthshaking to me and took me several months to find healing. At this time, my mom told me who my biological father was, and although I didn't know him personally, he'd been in close proximity to my family my entire life.

I decided at that point not to meet or reach out to him. My rationale wasn't only based on the pain I was feeling. I knew he had other kids, and I didn't want them to experience the total upheaval of their lives that I'd experienced.

A few years later, I received a call letting me know that my biological father had been diagnosed with terminal brain cancer. He had a few months to live, and if I ever wanted to meet him, it was time. So Trish and two of our three boys made the trip to the assisted-living facility and spent about two hours with him.

He sat with us and told us stories of his childhood, walked us through his high school yearbook, and showed us pictures of himself as a young man. He was genuine and his communication heartfelt. At the end of our time, he apologized for all I'd been through. All that was healing, but I still had a very big issue: I didn't think he was my father.

He was barely 5'9" and looked nothing like me. I am 6'3". As we went through his pictures, I saw no resemblance in him as a kid, no likeness to what I looked like in high school. Our hands weren't similar. Our facial structures were completely different. Walking out of the nursing home, I was convinced that he wasn't my dad.

Immediately after we got in the car, I called my mom and asked, "Who else was there? There had to have been someone else. This wasn't the guy." My mom was taken aback by my bluntness. She assured me that the man I had met in the nursing home was my biological father.

In the summer of 2021, I received a call that my uncle had passed away. My aunt asked if I would do the graveside service. I agreed. Because of my biological dad's proximity to my family, I knew my half brother and half sister would be at the funeral. I would meet them for the first time.

As I was walking to the head of the casket at the cemetery, a woman approached me with her hand extended and introduced herself as my sister. I quickly shook her hand and then opened my arms to offer a hug instead of a handshake. That embrace helped soften the awkwardness both of us were feeling in that moment. Later, at lunch, I got more acquainted with the brother and sister I hadn't met. I exchanged cell-phone numbers with my sister and left feeling some closure.

A few weeks later, the feeling I had when I met my biological father returned. I couldn't shake it. I didn't think he was my father. I texted my new sister and asked if she would do an ancestry DNA test with me. She agreed, and so I purchased two kits, and we both sent in our samples. About six weeks later, I got a text from her that her family tree had posted and asking if I'd received my results. My results were back as well. We weren't related. There was no hint of her on my family tree and no hint of me on her family tree. I felt devastated and validated all at the same time.

During this same timeframe, my wife did an ancestry DNA kit as well. Her maiden name is Lopez, so she was very interested in learning more about her Hispanic heritage. Before I got my results back, Trish received an email from the DNA-testing company that her family tree was ready to view. When she opened her DNA results, there was no trace of Mexican or Hispanic relatives, which was a surprise, because her dad is 100 percent Hispanic. At the time, we didn't really know what to make of it. We assumed that not enough of her relatives had taken ancestry DNA tests to accurately reflect her heritage.

The week after I got my results back, Trish had lunch with her dark hair, dark eyes, olive skin, Hispanic sister and told her my story and how I'd just found out, again, that my dad wasn't my dad. In a passing comment, Trish said, "Would you believe that I did an ancestry DNA test too, and it says that I am not Hispanic?" Her sister's eyes got really big, and she urged Trish to talk to her mom about the results.

The details of Trish's story are hers to share, but I can tell you this: in the span of ten days, both my wife and I found out that our dads weren't our biological fathers—me for the second time and Trish for a devastating first time. Identity has been a core wound we've had to navigate as a family.

finding your identity in Christ

If you are going to move past being perfect and be real, the journey of finding your identity, value, and worth in Christ is essential. Every day, there is an assault on your identity. It may not be as literal as what Trisha and I have experienced over the past few years, but what started in the garden with Adam and Eve continues to this day. It may be a commercial that says you'd look better with different clothes or a better body. It may be a comment someone makes to you that prompts you to compare yourself with another person. It may involve the loss of a job or a relationship. If the enemy can convince you that your identity and value can be found in something or someone other than God, then you will settle for a life far less than the life God has for you.

I love this statement from poet Johann Wolfgang von Goethe:

> If you treat an individual as he is, he will remain how he is. But if you treat him as if he were what he ought to be and could be, he will become what he ought to be and could be.[11]

Jesus was a master of treating people as they could be. One of my favorite interactions in the Gospels is between Jesus and a man known only as "a leper," in Luke 5. Leprosy was a physical disease and, to the Jewish people, a spiritual condition. Leprosy was a disease with no cure, and it had a social and spiritual stigma that put the inflicted person in isolation.

> While Jesus was in one of the towns, a man came along who was covered with leprosy. When he saw Jesus, he fell with his face to the ground and begged him, "Lord, if you are willing, you can make me clean."
>
> Jesus reached out his hand and touched the man. "I am willing," he said. "Be clean!" And immediately the leprosy left him. (Luke 5:12–13)

Leprosy is a skin disease that attacks and kills the flesh. After the skin is dead, the disease digs deeper and attacks the nerves. It is extremely painful, and people would break clay pots and dig at the skin with the broken pieces to try to relieve the pain.

But that wasn't the worst part. In Leviticus 13, God gave regulations about infectious diseases. Ceremonial cleanliness was central to the spiritual life of God's people. God decreed that those with leprosy were ceremonially unclean. This distinction meant they were excluded from the temple and even the camp, and by the time of Jesus, the religious leaders had taken it further and cast them from the city. Leper communities were established, two miles outside of the city gates.

But even that wasn't the worst part. No physical contact was allowed between a clean person and the unclean leper—no hugs, no handshakes, no life-exchange from one person to the other. But that still wasn't the worst part.

As a leper approached a ceremonially clean person, they had to announce their disease. The leper had to shout, "Unclean, unclean," letting everyone know they were untouchable. Their leprosy became their spiritual and relational identity.

We aren't too different from the leper. Their disease was on the outside, and ours is on the inside. Anger, lust, loneliness, gossip, lying, and jealousy can become the leprosy of our soul. Our sins and mistakes can become our identity.

Verse 12 says that this man was covered in leprosy. The implication was that, because it covered his entire body, he'd been a leper for a long time. His disease started out small and, over the course of time, had taken over his entire body. He'd probably lost fingers and may have been unrecognizable to his friends and family. The life he had dreamed of as a boy was not to be.

When the man with leprosy saw Jesus, something happened. He didn't announce his disease or cry out, "Unclean." Instead, he fell at Jesus' feet and said, "Lord, if you are willing, you can make me clean."

There was a lot going on in this declaration. First, he addressed Jesus as "Lord." The Jewish people believed that only God could heal. Somehow, without any proximity to people or the temple, this leper knew Jesus was Lord. He had a belief that Jesus' will aligned with God's will. Second, he said, "You can make me clean."

It's interesting that he didn't say, "You can heal me." In Jewish culture, the presence of a physical disability or illness was evidence of God's anger or judgment. There was a predominant belief that those with leprosy were being punished for their sins or the sins of their parents. So, this leper believed that, if Jesus made him clean spiritually, he would be healed physically.

Then, one of my favorite moments of Jesus' ministry happened: "Jesus reached out his hand and touched the man. 'I am willing,' he said. 'Be clean!' And immediately the leprosy left him" (Luke 5:13).

Why is this verse so significant? Jesus touched him—a person who hadn't been touched in years. A person who had lived in isolation, surrounded by death, decay, and disease, was touched by the hand of God. Jesus didn't have to touch him to heal him. He healed Jairus' daughter from another town. He raised Lazarus from the dead without going into the tomb. He healed the centurion's servant without a touch.

Why did He touch him? He touched him not to heal him but to give him worth. The words "Be clean" healed him. The leprosy didn't leave after the touch; they left after the words. Jesus' words restored his health and healed his skin; Jesus' touch restored his value and healed his heart.

The next part of this encounter is incredible: "Then Jesus ordered him, 'Don't tell anyone, but go, show yourself to the priest and offer the sacrifices that Moses commanded for your cleansing, as a testimony to them'" (Luke 5:14).

Why did Jesus tell him to go show himself to the priest? Because only those who were ceremonially clean could go to the temple and offer sacrifices with the priest. He was clean. He was new. He was redeemed. He was healed. He had a new identity.

three statements to reinforce your true identity

The same is true for you. Rediscovering your identity is simple, but it's not easy. Over the last few years, I've leaned into three statements that have helped redefine my worth and uncover my identity in a season of identity crisis. These aren't daily affirmations or self-help tactics. They are parts of the practice of defining our identity through the truth of God's Word and through the lens of how our heavenly Father sees us.

"I am new"

"Therefore, if anyone is in Christ, the new creation has come: The old has gone, the new is here!" (2 Cor. 5:17).

The leper didn't go back and live in the leper colony. You are not your past. You are not your failures. You are not your parents. You are not your sister. You are not your regrets. You are not your sin. You are not your divorce. You are not your weight. You are not your unemployment. You are not the choices someone else made for you. You are not your brokenness. You are not your bitterness. You are not your abuse. You are not your loneliness. You are not your marital status. You are not your tax bracket. You are not your crisis.

Henri Nouwen said this: "Self-rejection is the greatest enemy of the spiritual life because it contradicts the sacred voice that calls us the 'Beloved.' Being the Beloved constitutes the core truth of our existence."[12]

You are loved. You are forgiven. You are redeemed. You are called. You are chosen. You are set apart. You are valued. You are gifted. You are prized. You are reconciled. You are noticed. You are pursued. You are a child of the King. You are a co-heir with Christ. You are a royal priesthood. You are adored and cherished and treasured by the God of this universe. That is who you are.

"I am complete"

"Don't let anyone capture you with empty philosophies and high-sounding nonsense that come from human thinking and from the spiritual powers of this world, rather than from Christ. For in Christ lives all the fullness of God in a human body" (Col. 2:8–9 NLT).

Every day, people and messages will try to capture you with the empty philosophy that you are not complete. *You aren't complete until your marriage is healed. You aren't complete until you are married. You aren't complete until you have a new job. You aren't complete until you become a parent. You aren't complete until you have a bigger house, nicer office, different tax bracket. You aren't complete.*

In Christ, you are complete. You don't have to marry anyone, fix anything, achieve anything, prove anything to one day become complete. Your identity with God is secure through the person of Jesus Christ.

"I am God's masterpiece"

"For we are God's masterpiece. He has created us anew in Christ Jesus, so we can do the good things he planned for us long ago" (Eph. 2:10 NLT).

For centuries, a painting called *Christ Mocked* was believed to be missing. The painting was from the Florentine artist Cimabue and depicted part of the crucifixion of Jesus. But in 2019, it turned up in the kitchen of a ninety-year-old woman living in the French countryside.

The painting had been hanging above a hotplate in the kitchen until an auctioneer came to the woman's house to prepare for her move. According to CNN, the painting was valued at $6.5 million but sold at auction for $26.8 million, four times the expected price.[13]

The masterpiece was worth so much more than the kitchen in which it hung. Value isn't determined by what someone thinks something to be worth. Value isn't determined by an appraisal of value. Value is always determined by what someone is willing to pay. The woman didn't think the painting was worth more than just nice kitchen decor. The appraiser valued this masterpiece at $6.5 million. But someone saw it as so much more valuable that they paid four times its projected value.

> In Christ, you are complete. You don't have to marry anyone, fix anything, achieve anything, prove anything to one day become complete.

No matter what you think about yourself, God sees you as His masterpiece. You are so valuable to God that He paid the price of His Son's life to restore your identity and determine your worth. Your value and worth aren't determined by your performance or your self-esteem. Your value, worth, and identity are secured by what Christ did on the cross. He sealed your value and identity for all eternity.

You are new. You are complete. You are God's masterpiece. That is who you are.

part three

embracing
God's
preferred
picture of you

chapter 9

taking off our masks

authenticity costs you up front, but not as much as hiding costs over time

> *"How can we be loved if we're always hiding?"*
>
> Donald Miller, *Scary Close*

In October of 2022, reporter Louis Keene started an article outlining the chain of events surrounding NBA star Kyrie Irving's suspension for posting a controversial tweet.[1] Irving had posted a link to a movie that *Rolling Stone* called "venomously antisemitic."[2]

From there, the snowball of backlash and consequences began to roll. Brooklyn Nets owner, Joe Tsai, who was also Irving's boss, condemned the tweet. Two days later, Irving doubled down and refused to issue an apology. The next day, Irving deleted the tweet. The following day, Jewish fans sat courtside at a Brooklyn Nets game wearing "Fight Antisemitism" shirts.

As the days went on, the media's and former NBA players' outrage toward Irving grew. On November 3, in a press conference after the Nets' practice, Irving declined another opportunity to apologize or to denounce anti-Semitism. The same evening, the Brooklyn Nets suspended him for a minimum of five basketball games, costing him $251,000 per game, amounting to over $1 million in salary. After his suspension, Irving issued a statement on Instagram, apologizing for hurting people and taking responsibility for his comment.

The next day, November 4, Nike said they were cutting ties with Irving and would not release his new signature shoe. The following day, the Nets released a six-step process for Irving to return to basketball with the Brooklyn Nets:

- Apologize/condemn the movie
- $500,000 donation to an anti-hate cause
- Sensitivity training
- Antisemitic training
- Meet with ADL, Jewish leaders
- Meet with Nets owner Joe Tsai to demonstrate understanding

By November 20, 2022, Irving had satisfied all reinstatement conditions and returned to play for the Brooklyn Nets. The biggest question surrounding Irving's apology was, how sincere was it?

While we can never fully grasp the motives of someone else's heart, in Irving's case, it's notable that the apology only came after the received consequences. Was his apology sincere? We will truly never know.

What I do know is that it's easy to judge someone else's sincerity without evaluating my own authenticity. I find myself creating religious checklists to perform that don't always match the condition of my heart. My concern in those moments isn't heart transformation but outward appearance. I am naturally insincere.

The word *sincere* packs a lot of deep meaning in seven letters. *Merriam-Webster's* defines *sincere* as "wholehearted; an absence of hypocrisy."[3] *Cambridge Dictionary* defines *sincere* as "not pretending or lying."[4] Dictionary.com defines *sincere* as "free of deceit, hypocrisy, or falseness; genuine;

real."[5] Finally, *Collins Dictionary* gives this explanation of *sincere*: "being the same in actual character as in outward appearance."[6]

Boom. Mic drop. That gets to the heart of giving up being perfect in the pursuit of being real.

In his book *The Thing Beneath the Thing*, Steve Carter shared the origin of our English word *hypocrite*.

> An actor in that [Roman] culture was referred to as a *hupokrité*, from which we derived our familiar word, *hypocrite.*
>
> For the Romans, to be an actor was to be a hypocrite. And while this did not hold the same negative connotation it does for Americans today, some elements carry through. Essentially, acting is pretending to be someone you're not. Just as today's performers use special effects, stage makeup and props to create illusions that help an audience disappear into the story, ancient actors wore an array of masks to help them evolve into different characters. One definition of *hupokrité* is "one who sifts under a mask." Of course, the danger comes when we attempt to do this in our real lives too. We lose ourselves when we put on masks to keep our insecurities from view.[7]

Jesus talked about the spiritual implications of being a hypocrite. In Matthew 6, Jesus preached what many theologians call the greatest sermon of all time, the Sermon on the Mount. In Matthew 6:1, Jesus defined the motivation for hypocritical behavior: "Watch out! Don't do your good deeds publicly, to be admired by others, for you will lose the reward from your Father in heaven" (NLT).

Jesus went to the heart of our choice to be insincere. Every time we choose to allow our outward appearance to shine brighter than our character, our motivation isn't to grow our character but to impress others. Jesus gave some "quick hitters" aimed at relevant spiritual practices of the religious leaders of His day to illustrate what hypocrisy looks like:

- "When you give to someone in need, don't do as the hypocrites do—blowing trumpets in the synagogues and streets to call attention to their acts of charity!" (Matt. 6:2 NLT).
- "When you pray, don't be like the hypocrites who love to pray publicly on street corners and in the synagogues where everyone can see them" (Matt. 6:5 NLT)
- "And when you fast, don't make it obvious, as the hypocrites do, for they try to look miserable and disheveled so people will admire them for their fasting" (Matt. 6:16 NLT).

Jesus identified the ways religious leaders put on masks and played a part in His culture to impress others and hide their authentic selves.

the masks we wear to impress others

In *The Thing Beneath the Thing*, Carter identified masks that we wear to disguise our imperfections and impress others.

the performer mask

Carter said that those wearing the Performer Mask expect to find their identities in their achievements and successes.[8] When I left the church in 2005 because of the affair, I had no idea what I was going to do with the rest of my life. I had forfeited my opportunity to be a pastor, but I had no other job experience as an adult. I had no clue what to do, but I felt like part of my healing was simply doing the next right thing. To provide for our basic needs until I could figure out my next career, I went to P. F. Chang's to apply for a job. I was a huge P. F. Chang's fan and felt like, if I was going to wait tables, at least I'd love to eat the leftovers I would bring home at the end of the night. I was hired and asked if I could start the next day.

I went from speaking to over five hundred people each weekend to "Would you like white or brown rice?" It was humbling and humiliating all at the same time. It was exactly what I needed. One night as I was closing my section, I had a table of several high school students who had come in for dinner after their school dance. They were loud, rude, made a huge mess, and had hung out so long that I was one of the last servers to leave. After they finally left, I was under their table on my hands and knees, sweeping rice and crushed fortune cookies into a dustpan with my hands. When I was done, I looked at the table, and they had left me a $5 tip! I thought, *I am busting my butt cleaning up after these kids who couldn't care less about me. When was the last time I did this at home?* I worked at P. F. Chang's for a little over two months, and God used that time to deconstruct the Performer Mask I'd worn my entire life.

What about you? Do you find yourself wearing the mask of performance? Here are a few questions to help you identify this mask:

- What happens when I fail?
- What happens when someone demonstrates supe-
  riority over me?[9]
- How does someone else's win affect me?

the pleaser mask

We talked about people-pleasing in chapter 5, but I love how Steve Carter identified the second mask, the Pleaser Mask. People who wear the Pleaser Mask often fixate on solving other people's problems. They carry a heavy sense of responsibility on their shoulders to take care of everybody else, often at the expense of their own selves and souls.[10]

When Trish and I first got married, she wore the Pleaser Mask. She is a compassionate person. When we visited her family or mine, because of how she is wired, she would own the problems of all our family members. Her sister's financial situation became her financial situation. My sister's marriage problems became something for her to take on. A crisis her parents were navigating became her crisis to figure out. She would be emotionally exhausted because she would own their problems and stress.

When we hide behind the Pleaser Mask, pleasing others becomes more important than being our authentic selves. The Pleaser Mask diminishes our ability to help others because we become less of who we were created to be.

A couple of questions we've implemented to identify and take off the Pleaser Mask might be helpful for you:

- Is this burden/problem/crisis something I need to own?
- Am I violating personal boundaries by trying to be pleasing to this person?

the perfecter mask

The person wearing a Perfecter Mask usually has a hard time showing vulnerability. Perfecters believe the lie that they have to have it all together.[11]

When we started Hope City, one of our axioms was "You can belong before you believe." I said this statement every single week at the beginning of my message. It was a reminder that you belong no matter who you are, where you've been, or where you are in your relationship with God. You are welcome.

Shortly after we opened the church, a woman started coming on Sundays. She and her husband had gone through some marital problems, and she resonated with the authenticity of our church. He was a firefighter and worked most Sundays, but he came occasionally.

A few months later, she approached me in the church lobby and said, "You know who would love this church?"

"Who?" I responded.

"My son would love this church. He's fallen away from God, but I think he would love it here."

The first time I remember seeing her son was after a service in December. He introduced himself to me, and said, "My mom said I would love this church. She never told me you wore camouflage and Jordans. So that seals the deal."

Now before you think I was tapping into my dad's hunting roots or wearing Carhartt camo, I was wearing a Ralph Lauren polo camo shirt. It was as suburban as a camouflage shirt could get. But for Seth, it was a sign that he was welcome.

Over the next few months, Seth attended Hope City and brought his two little kids. They would give me high fives in the lobby on their way to class. I started having short conversations with Seth in the lobby after services and learned that he was going through some relational conflict with his girl-friend. His life was pretty complicated, and he struggled with depression. He was open about choices he'd made that he wished were different. But for the first time in a long time, he realized that he didn't have to be perfect to be loved by God. It was an incredible feeling to see someone take off the Perfecter Mask and start to see themselves as God sees them.

On a Tuesday night, I got a call that no pastor wants to receive. It was from Seth's mom. She shared that Seth had taken his own life. He was twenty-seven years old. She asked me if I'd be willing to do the funeral. I was humbled to serve the family in this way. As I spent time with the family to prepare for the funeral, his dad said something that resonated: "Seth wasn't perfect, but he was trying to figure it out."

Isn't that all of us? None of us are perfect, yet we wear ourselves out hiding behind the Perfecter Mask. The more we wear it, the more we miss out on being authentic.

Here are a few questions to ask yourself if you struggle with the Perfecter Mask:

- Who am I trying to impress in my quest to appear perfect?
- What is the worst that can happen if I don't do everything perfectly today?
- Do I believe God still loves me in spite of my imperfections?

the power mask

We usually associate power with pride, but pride is often a facade for insecurity. Several years ago, my boys went to my alma mater, Lincoln

Christian University, for a week of basketball camp. About halfway through the week, Micah called. I said hello and heard giggles on the other end. "Hello? Micah?" I said.

Then, out of the giggles, one son said sarcastically, "What's up, god?"

"How's it going, god?" another son blurted out.

One by one, over the next thirty seconds, they asked me silly questions and addressed me as "god."

Finally, I said, "What is going on? Why are you guys calling me that?"

"Dad, you're on speaker phone with Coach Kenny." Coach Kenny was my college basketball teammate. "Kenny told us that when you were in college, you introduced yourself to Mom for the first time by saying, 'Hi, I'm god.'" Now they were belly-laughing.

I said, "Well, I don't know if that is true."

Kenny butted in. "JD, don't lie to your boys. You know you told Trish, 'Hi, I'm god.'"

Elijah said, "Dad, why would you do that? That is such a bad pickup line."

Kenny answered for me: "Boys, your dad was just that cocky."

I was an arrogant jerk in college. I came across to others as confident and prideful. But the nineteen-year-old who introduced himself as God was trying desperately to hide behind the Power Mask, praying no one would see my insecurities. The person who introduced himself as God had been sexually abused, had lust issues, and was terrified he would never be enough. The person who introduced himself as God was nervous he wouldn't fit in or be liked. He was insecure and out of place.

Steve Carter said, "Power is just a mask, an attempt to veil someone's deep insecurity and detract from personal potholes."[12]

Do you wear the Power Mask? Here are few questions that may help:

- Am I hiding behind the Power Mask hoping to detract from the potholes I hope no one notices?
- Do I power up on people in my life to make myself feel better?
- Do I use my title or authority to demonstrate power at home or at work?

the pretender mask

Pretenders would rather deal with people saying their efforts were weak than allow themselves to be fully seen and known with all their imperfections and vulnerabilities.[13]

As Trisha and I travel and share our story, one of the most common questions I get from parents is "How open are you with your kids about your story, mistakes, mess-ups, and struggles?"

Every story is different, and while this isn't a parenting book, I think one of the easiest places to hide as a parent is behind the Pretender Mask.

Most of us believe that to be successful as parents, we have to hide our flaws from our kids. If we can appear perfect, then maybe our kids won't make the same mistakes we make. As a parent of three adult kids, I can confidently tell you that your kids don't need to see you pretending to be perfect. What your kids need most from you is authenticity.

Micah graduated high school from Christ Presbyterian Academy in Nashville, Tennessee. He had an incredible experience there. The Christian environment was a growth catalyst for him. As a part of the graduation ceremony, each student received a paragraph in the graduation program describing their character, written by their advisory teacher. In part, Micah's teacher said, "He is willing to admit his flaws and weaknesses."

Micah didn't feel the need to hide his imperfections. A few days after the graduation ceremony, I asked him about the quote. He shared that seeing Trish and my willingness to share our weaknesses and struggles with others gave him the freedom he needed not to pretend to be flawless.

We have good intentions when we hide our mistakes from our kids. We want them to respect us. We want them to look up to us. We want them to be proud of us. We don't want to trouble them. We don't want them to think we are weak. None of these are wrong desires. The problem is that deception never leads to freedom; it always leads to bondage.

A mistake kept hidden is often repeated.

I think this principle is why God shares so much of people's dysfunction and brokenness with us in the Bible. They were messed up. He didn't have to tell all those stories of betrayal, heartache, loss, bitterness, and adultery. He shared their mistakes so we wouldn't repeat them.

I'm not saying we should share *details* of our sins or bad choices with our kids. Your kids don't need to know how often you used to get drunk or the details of your dating life in high school. However, your kids need to know that you fail and mess up, and also see the process of confession, repentance, forgiveness, and restoration in front of them—they need to see you take off the Pretender Mask. Seeing you transformed by the grace and mercy of a loving God gives them hope that they don't have to pretend.

the meaning of Moses' "mask"

In Exodus 33, we find Moses in an intense conversation with God. Moses was instructed by God to climb Mount Sinai to receive from God the Ten Commandments. He came down with the tablets in hand to find the people of Israel melting gold to create idols to worship other gods. In frustration,

Moses threw down the Ten Commandment tablets and destroyed them. Moses hit a breaking point as a leader and retreated once again to have a conversation with God.

Because of his frustrations with the Israelites, God said He would send an angel with them into battle, but He would not personally go with them. He had tried to live in covenant with the nation of Israel, yet they continually opted for a contractual agreement. He wouldn't go back on His promise, but how He fulfilled His promise was about to change.

> Then the LORD said to Moses, "Leave this place, you and the people you brought up out of Egypt, and go up to the land I promised on oath to Abraham, Isaac and Jacob, saying, 'I will give it to your descendants.' I will send an angel before you and drive out the Canaanites, Amorites, Hittites, Perizzites, Hivites and Jebusites. Go up to the land flowing with milk and honey. But I will not go with you, because you are a stiff-necked people and I might destroy you on the way." ...
>
> Then Moses said to him, "If your Presence does not go with us, do not send us up from here. How will anyone know that you are pleased with me and with your people unless you go with us? What else will distinguish me and your people from all the other people on the face of the earth?" (Ex. 33:1–3, 15–16)

The Israelites might have missed the point, but Moses saw the bigger picture. He knew that without God it didn't matter what the Israelites did or didn't have. Nothing is better than the presence of God. God was impressed with Moses' boldness and request. So, God changed His mind and agreed to go with the Israelites into battle.

Moses then doubled down on the favor he'd found with God and made a request that only someone close to God could make. "Then Moses said, 'Now show me your glory'" (v. 18).

God's glory is greater than any human can sustain, so God put Moses in the cleft of a rock and placed His hand over Moses as He passed by. This was an act of grace and mercy by God not only to Moses but also to the people of Israel.

Chapter 34 of Exodus is the account of God giving Moses and the people of Israel a second chance and a new covenant. God instructed Moses to chisel out new tablets with his commandments.

> So Moses chiseled out two stone tablets like the first ones and went up Mount Sinai early in the morning, as the LORD had commanded him; and he carried the two stone tablets in his hands. Then the LORD came down in the cloud and stood there with him and proclaimed his name, the LORD. And he passed in front of Moses, proclaiming, "The LORD, the LORD, the compassionate and gracious God, slow to anger, abounding in love and faithfulness, maintaining love to thousands, and forgiving wickedness, rebellion and sin. Yet he does not leave the guilty unpunished; he punishes the children and their children for the sin of the parents to the third and fourth generation." (Ex. 34:4–7)

God's presence came down in the cloud and passed in front of Moses. It was a defining moment in the life of Moses. As Moses came down from

Mount Sinai, his face was glowing from being in the presence of God. The glory of God was on his face, so Moses put on a veil, a mask. "Then Moses would put the veil back over his face until he went in to speak with the LORD" (Ex. 34:35).

That is the backdrop for what the apostle Paul wrote to the Corinthian church:

> We are not like Moses, who would put a veil over his face to prevent the Israelites from seeing the end of what was passing away. (2 Cor. 3:13)

> But the people's minds were hardened, and to this day whenever the old covenant is being read, the same veil covers their minds so they cannot understand the truth. And this veil can be removed only by believing in Christ. Yes, even today when they read Moses' writings, their hearts are covered with that veil, and they do not understand.

> But whenever someone turns to the Lord, the veil is taken away. For the Lord is the Spirit, and wherever the Spirit of the Lord is, there is freedom. So all of us who have had that veil removed can see and reflect the glory of the Lord. And the Lord—who is the Spirit—makes us more and more like him as we are changed into his glorious image. (2 Cor. 3:14–18 NLT)

The word *mask* has a different weight in a post-Covid world than it did before March 2020. Whatever your opinion on masks, they became a part of our world's vernacular, economy, and social consciousness. Wearing a mask was required for every social aspect of our lives. Masks became such a part of our mainstream life that Apple provided iOS update 14.5 that recognized your Face ID while wearing a mask.[14]

Churches often used the mask mandate as an opportunity to connect the physical mask with a spiritual condition. A quick Google search of the term "Unmasked Sermon Series" returns 659,000 matches. Physical masks played a positive role in our physical health, but figurative masks compromise our spiritual, relational, and emotional health.

Masks never bring us closer to who we were created to be. They make shallow what God intended to be deep. Our friendships, marriages, families, churches—everything in our lives gets cheated when we choose to wear a mask.

> A mistake kept hidden
> is often repeated.

In 2 Corinthians 3:13, Paul said, "We are not like Moses, who put a veil over his face so the people of Israel would not see the glory, even though it was destined to fade away" (NLT).

I like Eugene Peterson's translation of this verse better, "Unlike Moses, we have nothing to hide. Everything is out in the open with us. He wore a veil so the children of Israel wouldn't notice that the glory was fading away—and they *didn't* notice" (MSG).

a mask only reveals part of reality

I always thought Moses put a mask on his face to protect the people of Israel from seeing God's glory. In Exodus 34:30–33, it says this:

> When Aaron and all the Israelites saw Moses, his face was
> radiant, and they were afraid to come near him. But Moses
> called to them; so Aaron and all the leaders of the commu-
> nity came back to him, and he spoke to them. Afterward
> all the Israelites came near him, and he gave them all the
> commands the LORD had given him on Mount Sinai.
>> When Moses finished speaking to them, he put a veil
> over his face.

Paul implied that Moses' veil wasn't intended to protect people from God's glory, but rather to keep them from seeing God's glory *fade away*. Moses' mask was meant to hide the truth that the glory of God was fading. Theologian Marvin Richardson Vincent said this: "What the veil prevented the Israelites from seeing, was the disappearance of the glory—the type of the termination of Moses' ministry."[15]

We do the same thing in our lives today. We have Snapchat and Instagram filters to mask our imperfections. We fear what people will think of us if we present a less-than-perfect version of ourselves. We want people to see us in all our glory.

As parents, Trish and I have tried not to pressure our kids to get certain grades. Our expectation is for them to do their best. Whatever their best is, that is acceptable to us. If your academic best is 4.0, awesome. If your best is 2.5, awesome. Just do your best. We measure effort, not outcomes. When we adopted our two younger kids, we had some adjustments to make to our parenting style and how involved we were in their academic lives, compared to our older kids'.

About halfway through our adoptive kids' first school semester with us, I got an email from Janiyah's teacher. She asked me about all the incomplete or uncorrected assignments she'd sent home with Janiyah that I hadn't signed and returned to the school. This was the first I'd heard of these papers.

When the kids got home from school, I immediately asked Janiyah about the assignments. She said, "All the papers are in my backpack."

I said, "Why haven't I seen these papers?"

She said, "I know you don't want to see that many papers with bad grades."

Masks allow us to only present an altered version of reality.

the mask that covers your face also covers your heart

What started out as a superficial cover-up for Moses became a spiritual condition.

> But the people's minds were hardened, and to this day whenever the old covenant is being read, the same veil covers their minds so they cannot understand the truth. And this veil can be removed only by believing in Christ. Yes, even today when they read Moses' writings, their hearts are covered with that veil, and they do not understand. (2 Cor. 3:14–15 NLT)

Brené Brown said, "Authenticity is a collection of choices that we have to make every day. It's about the choices to show up and be real. The choice to be honest. The choice to let our true selves be seen."[16]

When you wear a mask long enough, your heart becomes hardened to the person you were created to be. You start to accept what Brennan Manning called "impostors" as the real you. The longer you wear masks, the more distance you feel in your relationship with God.

The choice to take off our masks isn't a onetime thing. It is a daily choice we consciously make. Being real isn't a switch we flip. It's consistently choosing to take off our masks, be real, be vulnerable, and allow our true selves to be seen.

the maskless freedom you long for is found in Jesus

"But whenever someone turns to the Lord, the veil is taken away. For the Lord is the Spirit, and wherever the Spirit of the Lord is, there is freedom" (2 Cor. 3:16–17 NLT).

What I love about this verse is the word *wherever*. Every moment of every day, freedom is available. You can't earn it. You can't prove it. You don't deserve it. You aren't impressive enough for it. Whenever and wherever you turn to the Lord, the veil is taken away.

The Greek word Paul used in verse 16 for "taken" is the word περιαιρέω (*periaireó*), which means "is removed" or "is taken away." More important than the meaning of the word is the verb tense Paul used. The tense is present, passive, indicative, third person. What does that mean? It means that *you* can't take it away. It's taken away by the Lord. God takes it away as you turn to Him. You have a role to play, but your role is submission to God's desire for you to live maskless.

how to give God permission to remove your masks

To embrace God's preferred picture of you, you have a few crucial choices that give God permission to remove the mask you've grown accustomed to wearing.

admit to wearing a mask

The first choice you have to make is to admit you're wearing a mask. There are things about following Jesus that are simple but not easy. This is one of them. You have to come face to face (pun intended) with the areas of your life you cover up and admit you aren't being fully authentic.

In Luke 12, Jesus was talking to a massive crowd of people. His ministry had momentum, and people were coming to hear Him teach and see Him perform miracles. But in this passage, it says that Jesus had one group of people in mind as He taught—His disciples:

> By this time the crowd, unwieldy and stepping on each other's toes, numbered into the thousands. But Jesus' primary concern was his disciples. He said to them, "Watch yourselves carefully so you don't get contaminated with Pharisee yeast, Pharisee phoniness. You can't keep your true self hidden forever; before long you'll be exposed. You can't hide behind a religious mask forever; sooner or later the mask will slip and your true face will be known. (Luke 12:1–2 MSG)

Commentator Trent Butler said, "The hypocrite tries to cover up his life, not letting others see who he actually is. Jesus warned that this was impossible. God would bring their secret lives into the open."[17]

Author Donald Miller wrote this in his book *Scary Close*:

> It costs personal fear to be authentic but the reward is integrity, and by that I mean a soul fully integrated, no

difference between his act and his actual person. Having integrity is about being the same person on the inside that we are on the outside, and if we don't have integrity, life becomes exhausting.[18]

God loves you so much that He wants to set you free to live a life of integrity. When you are a disciple of Jesus, He doesn't want your life to look anything like the phoniness of the Pharisee. He wants you to be free. Freedom doesn't come without pain. But the pain of admitting you're wearing a mask is redemptive pain.

Are you exhausted from living an inauthentic life? The first step to freedom is admitting you're wearing a mask.

acknowledge the gap

The second choice you need to make is to acknowledge the gap between *me* and the *me I pretend to be*.

At the end of every year, I do an exercise that helps evaluate the level of authenticity I'm living in my relationship with God, my wife, and others. The exercise only works to the level of my willingness to be honest. It puts a quantitative value on the gaps of authenticity I have in my life. Here's how you can do it.

First, on a piece of paper, draw a continuum for each of the major areas of your life: spiritual, relational, emotional, marital (if you are married), parental (if you are a parent). Then, on one side of the continuum, write the word ME. On the other end of the continuum, write THE ME I PRETEND TO BE.

ME ———————————— THE ME I PRETEND TO BE
          100   75   50   25   0
                        SPIRITUAL

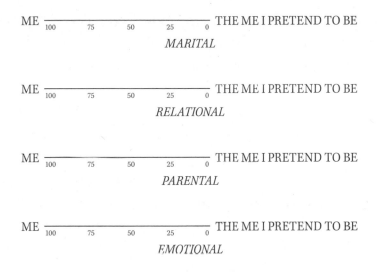

ME ————————————————— THE ME I PRETEND TO BE
   100   75   50   25   0
                MARITAL

ME ————————————————— THE ME I PRETEND TO BE
   100   75   50   25   0
               RELATIONAL

ME ————————————————— THE ME I PRETEND TO BE
   100   75   50   25   0
                PARENTAL

ME ————————————————— THE ME I PRETEND TO BE
   100   75   50   25   0
               EMOTIONAL

As you think about your life, your friendships, your marriage, your emotional life, your relationship with God, give yourself a score of 0 to 100, and write it on each line. Zero means *I am living a life of pretending—masked and fake.* One hundred (which I've never achieved) means *I am always the real me and never pretend or live with a mask.*

As you realize that brokenness isn't weakness, as you let go of people-pleasing and are brutally honest with God and give away your shame, you are able to close the gap between *me* and *the me I pretend to be.*

- How big is the gap in your marriage?
- How big is the gap in your friendships?
- How big is the gap in your relationship with God?

allow others to know the real you

Finally, to allow God to remove your masks, you have to let others know the real you. Donald Miller went on to say, "I wonder how many people get tempted by the gains they can make by playing a role, only to pay for those temptations in public isolation."[19]

Isolation is an enemy of transformation. The more we retreat and isolate, the less we will experience transformation.

I've quoted James 5:16 many times, but only in recent years have I understood its context and power: "Confess your sins to each other and pray for each other so that you may be healed" (NLT).

James commanded us to confess our sins, not to God, but to one another. Confession is not for forgiveness but for healing. The implication is that healing only comes as we confess our sins to one another.

You were created for relationships. Part of an authentic biblical relationship is a willingness to confess your sins to another person. This isn't for the purpose of finding or receiving God's forgiveness. That is a different kind of confession.

In 1 John 1:9, we read, "If we confess our sins, he is faithful and just and will forgive us our sins and purify us from all unrighteousness."

> Isolation is an enemy of transformation. Authenticity is the pathway to transformation.

Confession for the forgiveness of sins can only be done through what Jesus Christ did on the cross. But the soul-level healing and transformation we desire only comes as we identify the masks we wear, acknowledge the gaps in our lives, and allow others to know the real *me*. When we stop hiding, God can start healing.

Theologian J. Ronald Blue said this about James 5:16: "A mutual concern for one another is the way to combat discouragement and downfall. The cure is in personal confession and prayerful concern. The healing (that you may be healed) is not bodily healing but healing of the soul."[20]

> You can't overcome your porn addiction until you confess it.
> You can't get over your jealousy until you tell someone about it.
> You can't find healing from your abuse by suffering in silence.
> You can't mend your marriage until you tell someone it's broken.
> You can't find victory over your anger until you confess it's a problem.
> You can't get your drinking under control by trying harder; you have to tell someone.

Confess your sins to one another, that you may be healed.

Being real will cost you something. Not being real will cost you more. Being real isn't safe; it's risky. Being real isn't always popular. Being real is always worth it. Pastor Craig Groeschel said, "We may impress people with our strengths but we connect with people through our weaknesses."[21]

Here is how Paul concluded chapter 3 of 2 Corinthians: "So all of us who have had that veil removed can see and reflect the glory of the Lord. And the Lord—who is the Spirit—makes us more and more like him as we are changed into his glorious image" (2 Cor. 3:18 NLT).

Having the veil removed allows you to reflect the glory of God. As you do, God's commitment is transformation. You are changed into more of His glorious image as He removes your masks. Authenticity is the pathway to transformation.

chapter 10

living a transformed life

God doesn't use perfect people; He uses authentic people

> *"If we conceal our wounds out of fear and shame, our inner darkness can neither be illuminated nor become a light for others."*
>
> Brennan Manning, *Abba's Child*

August 2022 was my last counseling session with my counselor, Brian. I found this out when I arrived. I sat on the couch, and Brian said, "Before we get going, I have to tell you something. Today will be our last counseling session."

I was surprised because I didn't feel like I was whole. I was a year out from discovering (again) that my dad wasn't my dad and Trisha's dad wasn't her dad. Also, I was only four months removed from the church's closing. I'd come a long way, but I felt I had a long way to go.

I said, "Okay, I guess that is good, right? Do you think I've made so much progress that we have gone as far as we can?"

With a familiar sarcasm I'd grown to appreciate, he said, "No way. You are still really messed up and need a lot more help! This is our last counseling session because I'm done being a counselor."

I was shocked. "Wow. I'm sure this is my fault. My life is so broken you are retiring from counseling because I've brought you to the end of your ability to help. I've pushed you into retirement, haven't I?"

"No, you can't take credit for this. I'm leaving to write country-music jingles and personalized wedding songs for couples." When I realized he wasn't joking, I was speechless.

Then I finally said, "That's quite the leap. I didn't see that coming."

He gave me the backstory on how he had started doing this on the side, and it was getting to a place where he could not just supplement his income but replace it with this new venture.

I said, "So let me get this straight. I have abandonment issues. My mom has abandoned me; my dad of thirty-six years wasn't my real dad; another man I thought was my dad wasn't my dad after all, and I am now searching Ancestry.com for my real dad. My entire church has left me, and we've closed the doors. I pay you to be my friend and spend two hours per month with me, and now you are leaving me too? How are you leaving me any better than when I started with you? I will need counseling because of my counselor."

His response is why I miss him so much as my counselor: "You can't pay me enough to be your friend. I can make more writing jingles."

Fair enough. I said, "Well, you're on the clock now, so this session better be good."

As we put the sarcasm aside, he said something to start our last session together that I've thought about every day since that August afternoon. "You have been lied to, betrayed, or abandoned by every significant person in your life other than your wife. You can allow that to define you or refine you. It *will* change you. How it changes you is up to you."

the need for heart transformation

We equate transformation with being fixed. It's a linear procedure with a starting point, a predictable process, and an ending. If we can heal ourselves, then everything will be better. Can I share something with you? God doesn't want to fix you; He wants to transform your heart. Unfortunately, heart transformation doesn't happen as neatly and predictably as being fixed.

Life is an accumulation of sins, hurts, and disappointments. Maybe you were raped in high school. Maybe you had a one-night stand in college. Maybe you were physically or sexually abused as a kid. Maybe you had an abortion. Maybe you cheated on your first wife and are now married to the woman with whom you cheated. Maybe your dad left when you were a kid. Maybe someone said you were fat when you were ten, and you've felt fat ever since. Maybe you were fired from your dream job.

What I am learning is the amount of transformation I am capable of experiencing is in direct proportion to my willingness to understand my hurts and completely surrender them to the redeeming power of Christ. God promises to re-create you—that is how committed to your transformation He is. God doesn't want you to be better; He wants you to be brand-new.

> And I will give you a new heart, and I will put a new spirit in you. I will take out your stony, stubborn heart and give you a tender, responsive heart. (Ezek. 36:26 NLT)

> And the one sitting on the throne said, "Look, I am making everything new!" (Rev. 21:5 NLT)

> Put on your new nature, and be renewed as you learn to know your Creator and become like him. In this new life, it doesn't matter if you are a Jew or a Gentile, circumcised or uncircumcised, barbaric, uncivilized, slave, or free. Christ is all that matters, and he lives in all of us. (Col. 3:10–11 NLT)

A few years ago, Trish wanted to mulch the flower beds in our front yard. It was blazing hot outside; the last thing I wanted to do was landscape. As I've mentioned, I'm not too fond of manual labor. I'd rather hire someone to do this task, but Trish loves landscaping, so I saw it as an opportunity to be a good husband and build into my marriage.

I went to Home Depot and bought twelve bags of mulch. As I was unloading them, I noticed something that I thought was odd. She wasn't just removing the old mulch from the flower beds to prepare for the new mulch (like I would have done); she was taking a shovel and digging up by the roots every weed and every blade of grass. At one point, I said, "That seems like a lot of work."

She said, "If I don't dig it up, it will just come right back."

This is a principle that has been so true in my life. So often, I have settled for removing what was visible above ground. I have noticed a problem, realized a sin issue, faced a character flaw, and have been content to cut it off at ground level. The problem is, it just comes right back.

Here is the tension: digging below ground level costs you. Uncovering the root of your addiction, anger, lust, divorce, affair, debt, or dysfunctional dating life is painful.

Many of us encounter pain, embarrassment, or shame from a mistake that is visible to others, and we do our best to address it. We admit it. We tell our small group. We go to a few counseling sessions and find an accountability partner. We get porn-blocking software for our computers. We take an anger-management class. We stop dating for six months so we can get healthy. We manage the pain of the consequences of our mistakes.

We promise we'll never do that again, never give in to that again, never choose that again, never be tempted by that again, never compromise that again.

In our hearts, we mean it. Then a few days, weeks, or months later, we find ourselves back in the place we promised we'd never be. Simply settling for the pain of our consequences impairs our desire to pursue the greater pain of healing and transformation.

So many people wear themselves out merely trying to fix their problems, when God longs to transform their hearts. Maybe that is where you are as you read this book. You are tired. You are exhausted. You have tried everything you know to be a better husband, but it isn't enough. Maybe you have tried everything you can to make your kids happy, but it isn't enough.

You've exhausted yourself trying to stop, trying to get better, trying to "be a good Christian." Things improve for a week or a month or a year, but then you come back to this place of discouragement or discontentment. For something to be restored, it must be torn apart. But most of the time, we don't desire transformation as much as we do pain-free living.

So we struggle with the same things repeatedly; we fall into the same dysfunctional friendships, relationships, and marriages. We make the same promises continually and wonder why God isn't powerful enough to help us overcome our issues.

Author Jennie Allen said this in her book *Nothing to Prove*:

> Enjoying His grace does cost us something. One thing: death. Death of our old selves. Death of our pride. Death of thinking we can be enough on our own. It's hard; it's messy. You will hate it for a moment. But you know what happens in your soul? You get free.[1]

The life you long for is available. However, it comes with the cost of going below ground level and digging to the root. It will take more time. It will cost you more. It will be more painful than you can ever imagine. But the pursuit of this pain will lead to authentic life.

what stands in the way of transformation

What hinders the transformation of our hearts and pushes us to pursue being "fixed" is our tendency toward self-preservation.

sin management

I can't quantify how much of my Christian life has been wasted equating a transformed heart with how well I could manage my sin. One of the great tragedies in the church today is that we've too often reduced our relationship with God to a checklist of what we can do to manage or avoid sin, rather than focusing on who we can become as Christ transforms us.

Most of us don't struggle with new sins. There aren't any brand-new temptations we've never experienced before that threaten to take us out all at once. Instead, we get caught up in the same few sins over and over and over again.

If you're anything like me, your response to your most repeated sin is "That was the last time."

- That was the last time I used that credit card.
- That was the last time I talked to my wife like that.
- That was the last time I cussed at my kids.
- That was the last time I looked at porn.
- That was the last time I flirted with my coworker.
- That was the last time I hid that purchase from my husband.

"That was the last time" becomes famous last words of sin management. We do our best to manage our sin or, if we are superspiritual, to avoid it all together.

In his book *Finding God*, Dr. Larry Crabb talked about desire not as something to avoid but as something to embrace.

> When the subject of passion comes up, most of us imme-
> diately think of strong desires within us that we wish
> weren't there. The enemy has become dark desires—lust,
> worry, anger, and the like—and the power of the enemy,
> we assume, is the self-hatred and shame we've learned in
> dysfunctional communities.
>
> But perhaps bad passions are strong because good
> passions are weak. Maybe the problem is not too much
> desire, but rather too little. The core problem with most of
> us, including the sex addict, the workaholic, and the vic-
> tim of childhood abuse, is not that we are too passionate
> about bad things, but that we are not passionate enough
> about good things.[2]

What if one of the keys to experiencing transformational change isn't found in the energy you put into avoiding or managing sin, but rather in increasing your pursuit of God? Desiring more of God always leads to desiring sin less.

pain avoidance

The problem with transformation is that it usually starts with affliction. Jeremiah said in Lamentations 3:1, "I am the man who has seen affliction by the rod of the LORD's wrath."

When the Babylonians destroyed Jerusalem and exiled its people to a distant country, they left Jeremiah behind. Jeremiah is known as the "weeping prophet" for good reason: he experienced the destruction of his city and mourned what he saw happen. This is the context of the book of Lamentations, a five-chapter song of sadness over what happened to Jeremiah's beloved city. But despite the horrible events that Jeremiah witnessed, he was still able to say, "The faithful love of the LORD never ends! His mercies never cease. Great is his faithfulness; his mercies begin afresh each morning" (Lam. 3:22–23 NLT).

Author C. S. Lewis said, "God whispers to us in our pleasures, speaks in our conscience, but shouts in our pains: it is his megaphone to rouse a deaf world."[3]

Often, God's path to healing and transformation involves pain. The reason we experience little transformation is because we have equated numbness with contentment. But living a numb life only prevents us from becoming the people God longs for us to be. I like avoiding pain more than I like change. But unfortunately, change usually requires pain. Most of my life's transformation seasons initially started with tremendous pain or discomfort—personal failure, financial hardship, job transition, marriage problems, relationship issues. When we begin to value avoiding pain more than we value transformation, we are guaranteed to stay the same.

Why do we repeatedly make promises that we intend to keep but don't? Why do we desire to be different but only experience incremental transformation?

incremental change

Incremental change is doing your best and working your hardest to stay married or to not get divorced. Incremental change makes big promises but lasts only a short time. Incremental change is change you are in control of. Incremental change is you working harder to stop the things you keep messing up. Incremental change, at its core, has you at the center trying to be better today than you were yesterday. Incremental change tells you if you try hard enough, you can cuss less, drink less, click on pornography less, eat less, lose your temper less, spend less, lust less, lie less, cheat less. Incremental change is motivated by guilt and shame and feelings of incompetence and failure. Incremental change convinces you that if you can endure the pain of trying harder to cover up your sin and get better, then no one needs to know; you can overcome this. Incremental change doesn't allow you to experience grace and forgiveness because you are constantly trying to make up for the sin in your life. Incremental change carries a small price tag up front, but it robs you for the rest of your life of the peace and joy and victory God longs to provide.

the difference of transformational change

There is another option. God offers transformational change. Transformational change is about surrender, vulnerability, and transparency; humility and dependency. Transformational change at its core aims to destroy you, and if you are willing to pay that price, it will dismantle every part of you. Transformational change is messy and bloody. It hurts deep, and it will cost you everything. It is pulling all your junk out and laying it on the table for all to see and not caring what they think about you. Transformational change is committed not just to dealing with the symptoms of your issues, but to peeling back painful layer after painful layer of your past, your dysfunction, and your sin, until the core problem is exposed. Transformational change is recognizing that on your best day, you are a failure and a sinner, and that your only hope is grace. Transformational change is knowing you can never try hard enough to overcome your desire to drink, cuss, lust, gorge, lie, and cheat. What you can do is surrender to the God of resurrection power, allowing Him not only to destroy you but to also bring you back to life. To be brought back to life, one first has to die.

Humans have created incremental change because we don't like the pain of transformational change.

You don't need incremental change in your relationship with God; you need transformational change. You don't need an improved version of the old you; you need a brand-new you. You don't need a slight improvement in your relationship with God; you need a complete transformation. The great news is that God offers to transform you. God offers to give you a new life.

I bet you want to change. You want to be different. I know that is the desire of your heart. You want a different marriage. You wish your relationships with your kids were different. You want to stop whatever it is you can't stop. I do too.

The bad news is that it will come at a severely high price—your complete self. But the life you will have on the other side of confession, repentance, pain, forgiveness, and surrender will be the life you have been pretending to have all the years you have tried to change a little at a time. Transformation is possible, but it has requirements.

While the process of transformation is not linear, it is foreseeable. By that I mean, God uses a repeated approach to bring transformational change to our lives. Here is the best way I've found to articulate this process in my life:

- Recognize what needs transformed.
- Confess to someone.
- Stop trying harder and surrender more.
- Take the next step of obedience.
- Repeat each step as necessary.

I am writing this chapter the first week of December 2022. It has been a little over seven months since the church closed. One of the commitments I made to my family and to God is that I'd do my best to process my feelings of failure, grief, and regret well and ask God to use the closing of the church to transform me.

I can't calculate how many dollars and hours I've spent being true to my promise—individual counseling, group counseling, one-on-one meetings with mentors, a LifePlan retreat in Colorado, books read, journals filled with prayers. I'm not trying to brag, but I got this right. God has transformed one of the most painful situations in my life into what I can see as a gift and a blessing now.

So, imagine my surprise this past Sunday when I walked into the church we've been attending and felt a level of grief like I haven't experienced since the last Sunday of Hope City Church. The Christmas decorations, the Christmas carols we sung as worship songs, the Christmas sermon, all hit me hard. I had to get up in the middle of the service to go to the bathroom to collect myself. I could have curled up in a fetal position and cried for hours if I wasn't in public.

We left the service and went to lunch and I was a shell of myself. I was trying to process what I was feeling and at the same time wondering what was wrong with me that I felt so much grief. I shared with Trish the emotional roller coaster I was on and could see on her face she was sitting next to me on the ride. She was hurting too.

A few hours later, I wrote this post on Facebook:

> Walking into church today, I was overwhelmed by grief in a way I haven't felt since we closed the church in April.
> Christmas was a special time at Hope City. I miss our staff. I miss our church. I miss my friends. I miss meeting

new people during the first week of a Christmas series. I
miss dreaming about and planning for Christmas Eve. I
will miss standing onstage with my family on Christmas
Eve, singing "Silent Night."

Immediately the shame of feeling sad flooded my
thoughts: "You shouldn't feel sad; you should be over this."

But I guess I'm not over it ... and that's ok. I discovered another part of my heart and story I need to give to
Jesus. He can be trusted.

So, if you are grieving the loss of something or someone in your life, I see you. I feel you. You are not alone. The
only way over your grief is to go through it.

Here are some thoughts on grief that are helping me
today:

- Grief comes in layers and waves. Healing comes by
  peeling back the next layer, acknowledging it, and
  giving it to God.
- You can be devastated by what was lost and excited
  about what is next at the same time. Feeling grief
  over a loss indicates how much it really meant to
  you.
- No one can dictate your path to healing. It's your
  journey, timetable, and heart.
- The only way to get over it is to go through it. There
  are no shortcuts to healing.

You're going to be ok. We're going to be ok.

Transformation is a process. Sin isn't the only thing that needs transformed in our lives. Grief, pain, regret, sadness, loss. God longs to transform all of the heart. But nothing can be transformed without recognizing it. We have to identify what needs transformation. That is the first step in the process.

For me, the next step is confession. I've never healed from a pain I haven't confessed. I've never overcome a sin I haven't admitted. We talked about the importance of confession in the previous chapter, but I think it's important to revisit this topic as it relates to transformation.

In the American Church, we've equated accountability with confession and transparency. When Trisha and I married and entered the ministry in 1995, I prided myself on being accountable. I was accountable in my choices: I wouldn't counsel a woman behind a closed office door or give a teenage girl a ride home from church without another person in the car. I would only do lunch with a woman if my wife or another man were with us. At all costs, I wanted to be accountable.

When we started Genesis Church in 2002, I knew accountability would be essential. So, I sought out a guy in our core group and asked him if we could meet each Wednesday morning to "hold each other accountable."

As a church planter, I had a church-planting coach. He and I would meet every Thursday morning. He asked me questions about my relationship with God. He asked me questions about my marriage, my struggles, and my weaknesses. He wanted to hold me accountable.

I had a group of elders that I met with once a month. They were the spiritual leaders of our church, and I was accountable to them. So, with all of these boundaries, safeguards, and great leaders and friends holding me accountable, how could I ever be unfaithful to God and my wife? That wasn't possible. But I was unfaithful, despite all my accountability.

What I have discovered is accountability is useless. Accountability is only as valuable as the transparency you and I offer in the context of that accountability.

It is easy for me to fake you out. It is easy for you to lie to my face. It is easy to pretend your marriage is better than it is. It is easy to offer just enough accountability to make yourself look spiritual.

But at the same time, partial accountability can be so dangerous because you are not only fooling me, you are fooling yourself as well. The truth is you and I can meet every Wednesday, and I can lie to you. You can have several circles of accountability, but unless you are 100 percent transparent in at least one of those circles, your heart won't experience the transformation you desire.

I am not saying you should be 100 percent transparent with everyone, but you should be 100 percent transparent with someone.

I have two people in my life who can ask me anything and I give them 100 percent of the truth; I withhold nothing. So, if I am struggling or need to confess something or am in a dark place, I can share that with these two people.

We can't substitute accountability for transparency. Accountability without transparency is useless. Of course, it is easier in the short term to offer accountability, and it seems more spiritual. But you experience more of God's grace and transformation when you offer transparency. When you are willing to offer transparency, you will find you don't need to be "held accountable."

Brennan Manning wrote this in *Abba's Child*:

> Only in a relationship of the deepest intimacy can we
> allow another person to know us as we truly are. It is

difficult enough for us to live with the awareness of our stinginess and shallowness, our anxieties and infidelities, but to disclose our dark secrets to another is intolerably risky. The impostor does not want to come out of hiding. He will grab for the cosmetic kit and put on his pretty face to make himself "presentable."[4]

There is no transformation without confession.

> Accountability is only as valuable as the transparency you and I offer in the context of that accountability.

The next step in the process of transformation is to stop trying harder and surrender more. I heard Pastor Rick Warren say one time, "Most Christians think they become more like Christ by trying, but it's actually by dying."

The apostle Paul said, "For you died, and your life is now hidden with Christ in God" (Col. 3:3).

You can't do anything to make God love you more. You can't do anything to make God love you less. God accepts you as you are, not because of what you've done for Him, but because of what Jesus did on the cross. It was the cross of Jesus that gave you the forgiveness of sins, eternal life, and the right to be called a son or daughter of God. Maybe you are tired from trying to earn favor with God. Trying to be a good person. Trying to do more good things in your life than bad. Trying not to sin. Trying to fix your life.

Maybe the best thing you can do this morning isn't to try harder, but simply to surrender more.

Do you have an "I will never" list?

- I will never lose my temper again.
- I will never go on Tinder again.
- I will never drink that much again.
- I will never talk to my kids like that again.
- I will never watch that again.
- I will never have a one-night stand again.

Surrender is about giving up "I will never" in favor of "I will surrender."

- God, I surrender my anger to you.
- God, I surrender my dating life to you.
- God, I surrender my sexuality to you.
- God, I surrender my drinking problem to you.
- God, I surrender my speech to you.
- God, I surrender my porn problem to you.
- God, I surrender my insecurity issues to you.

Transformation is found at the intersection of God's power and our surrender.

The next choice in the process of transformation is taking the step into obedience. We can identify the areas of our lives that need change. We can confess to God and to our closest friends the sins we struggle with or the grief we need to have healed. We can surrender those to the Lord over and over again, but without obedience, there is no transformation. Nothing changes until we obey God.

Romans 6:16 says: "Don't you know that when you offer yourselves to someone as obedient slaves, you are slaves of the one you obey—whether you are slaves to sin, which leads to death, or to obedience, which leads to righteousness?"

Look at anyone whom God used in extraordinary ways in Scripture. God brought radical transformation through their obedience. It was as they said "Yes" to God that they lived a transformed life—Abraham, Noah, Moses, Joshua, Esther, David, Daniel, Mary, Simon Peter, Paul. The prerequisite to transformation was obedience.

Maybe you're waiting on God to transform your marriage, but you aren't obeying God's call to be a loving husband.

Maybe you are waiting on God to change your financial situation, but you've done nothing to be obedient to Him in your finances. You are in debt, and don't tithe. You spend above your means, but you're waiting for transformation.

Maybe you're asking God to transform your marital status because you are lonely and tired of being single, but you continue to date people who pull you further from God.

Maybe you're waiting on God to transform a relationship, but you haven't been obedient in offering forgiveness.

You keep waiting on God to transform your career situation, but you aren't being obedient in the job you have now.

God brings transformation *through* our obedience, not before our obedience. Delayed obedience is disobedience. Is there an area of your life you need transformational change but have been unwilling to be obedient?

The final step in the process of transformation is to repeat any of the previous steps as necessary. As I discovered last Sunday, transformation is more like an onion than an apple. An apple has one layer and a core. An onion has several layers that often induce tears as you peel them back. You may have to confess something a few times before you're ready to surrender it. You may have to surrender something to God multiple times before you have the courage to obey. You may have to choose to obey God in different ways before you notice the transformation He brings.

The nation of Israel was rescued by God at the crossing of the Red Sea. The obedience required for God to part the water was one man raising his staff toward heaven. Forty years later, the crossing of the Jordan into the Promised Land required twelve men to step into the waters at flood stage. Different seasons of life sometimes require new levels of obedience.

It's easy to get discouraged when it comes to change and transformation and to focus on how far you have to go and not on how far you've come. There are many areas of my life in which I am not where I want to be, but by God's grace, I am not where I used to be. God has changed me. I am different. How can you know if you are living a life transformed by God? Transformation isn't a formula to be learned but a process to be engaged, evaluated, and repeated.

a new way of measuring spiritual growth

One of the major objectives of our journey together in the first nine chapters of this book was to evaluate how we measure spiritual growth. For many of us, we've been told that you measure your relationship with God by how faithful you are with spiritual disciplines. Are you reading your Bible? Are you praying? Are you fasting? Are you journaling? Are you worshipping?

It is clear that our methods of measurement aren't effective. All of us know people who are at church every week, serve in the nursery, can say the books of the Bible in order from memory, and have a high knowledge of Jesus—but look nothing like Jesus. People are going to church, but they aren't changing.

Spiritual disciplines are important, but more information doesn't always lead to transformation. A few years ago, I started measuring the transformation in my life by a different standard.

Galatians 5:22–23 says, "But the fruit of the Spirit is love, joy, peace, patience, kindness, goodness, faithfulness, gentleness, self-control; against such things there is no law" (ESV).

A transformed life is more loving. A transformed life is more joyful. A transformed life is growing in kindness, goodness, and faithfulness. A transformed life is gentle and self-controlled.

If I am recognizing the things in my life that need to be transformed; if I am confessing those things to God and a trusted friend; if I am surrendering those things to Jesus and obeying what God asks of me—my life will be transformed to bear the fruit of the Spirit.

When we talk about Galatians 5:22–23, we often mistakenly say, "*fruits* of the Spirit." But the Greek word *karpos* is singular, masculine, and nominative. There are two observations about this Greek word. First, these aren't multiple fruits; this is one fruit. These character traits are one fruit of God's Holy Spirit transforming your heart. Most powerfully, the nominative tense of this word matters a great deal. The nominative is the case that normally refers to the subject of a verb or a noun following a form of the verb "to be" or "to become" (i.e., a predicate nominative) that renames the subject.[5]

The way that Paul wrote the word *fruit* literally means "to become." There is a transformative meaning baked into the word itself. The word *fruit* assumes that, as you walk with Jesus, a natural by-product is you will become a person of love, joy, peace, patience, kindness, goodness, faithfulness, gentleness, and self-control.

become a wounded healer

I was first introduced to the concept of a Wounded Healer while reading *Abba's Child* by Brennan Manning. Manning said this:

> In a futile attempt to erase our past, we deprive the community of our healing gift. If we conceal our wounds out of fear and shame, our inner darkness can neither be illuminated nor become a light for others. We cling to our bad feelings and beat ourselves with the past when what we should do is let go. But when we dare to live as forgiven men and women, we join the wounded healers and draw closer to Jesus.[6]

Transformation finds its ultimate purpose when you allow God to use your healed wounds to bring healing to others. What if God wants to leverage your past, your hurts, your sins, your mistakes, and your regrets to help others find healing and transformation?

Don't think it's possible? We see this over and over again in the ministry of Jesus in the Gospels.

In Matthew 9, Jesus went on a healing spree. He healed a sick woman and a dead girl. As He was leaving the home of the girl He raised to life, Matthew said that two blind men started following Him and calling out to Him, "Have mercy on us, Son of David!" They followed Jesus long enough that Jesus went to them and asked them if they truly believed He could restore sight.

"Yes, Lord," they replied.

So, Jesus touched them and healed them. Then, it says this in Matthew 9:30–31: "And their sight was restored. Jesus warned them sternly, 'See that no one knows about this.' But they went out and spread the news about him all over that region."

Remember, in that culture, physical disabilities were an indication of a spiritual deficiency. What was the first thing they did after Jesus healed them and then "sternly commanded" them not to tell anyone? They went and spread the news about Him all over the place—Wounded Healers!

In Mark 1, Jesus was approached by a man on his knees who was afflicted with leprosy. The man begged Jesus for a miracle. Jesus was filled with compassion and healed the man. We talked in chapter 8 about the significance of leprosy being healed. Once again, Jesus issued a command:

> Jesus sent him away at once with a strong warning: "See that you don't tell this to anyone. But go, show yourself to the priest and offer the sacrifices that Moses commanded for your cleansing, as a testimony to them." Instead he went out and began to talk freely, spreading the news. As a result, Jesus could no longer enter a town openly but stayed outside in lonely places. (Mark 1:43–45)

"Do not tell anyone about this." His first act after being made right with God was to disobey God. He couldn't help but be a Wounded Healer.

In Mark 7, Jesus was traveling to the Sea of Galilee. As He was on His journey, people brought Him a man who was deaf and could barely talk. His friends begged Jesus to heal him. Jesus took him away from the crowds, placed His fingers in the man's ears, and spit on the man's tongue. Then, the man could hear and speak plainly. Jesus responded in this way:

Jesus commanded them not to tell anyone. But the more
he did so, the more they kept talking about it. People were
overwhelmed with amazement. "He has done everything
well," they said. "He even makes the deaf hear and the
mute speak." (Mark 7:36–37)

What would you do if you couldn't hear or speak but then Jesus healed
you so you could hear and speak? He could finally talk, and the only thing
he wanted to talk about was Jesus, who healed him. He was a Wounded
Healer.

Let's go back to the story of the Samaritan woman at the well that we
talked about in chapter 2. I intentionally omitted a detail of her story for this
moment right here. In chapter 2, we left off with verse 28 of John 4: "Then,
leaving her water jar, the woman went back to the town and said to the
people, 'Come, see a man who told me everything I ever did. Could this be
the Messiah?' They came out of the town and made their way toward him"
(John 4:28–30).

The Samaritan woman went back to her village and said, "This guy just
told me everything I ever did. He has to be the Messiah."

Look how this story ends:

Many of the Samaritans from that town believed in him
because of the woman's testimony, "He told me everything I ever did." So when the Samaritans came to him,
they urged him to stay with them, and he stayed two days.
And because of his words many more became believers.

They said to the woman, "We no longer believe
just because of what you said; now we have heard for

ourselves, and we know that this man really is the Savior
of the world" (John 4:39–42).

Jesus stayed in a Samaritan village for two days because of this woman
who had been married five times and was living with a guy who wasn't her
husband. She was at the well at noon to avoid people. Because of her testimony, "many more became believers." She was a Wounded Healer.

Jesus didn't wait till she was in a stable relationship before He used her.
He didn't ask her to fix all aspects of her past before He used her. He didn't
ask her to go to a Bible study or to theologically explain the history of Jewish
and Samaritan worship before He used her. She was a Wounded Healer.

God can use your biggest failures, mistakes, and regrets as the launch-
ing pad to your greatest calling.

A few years ago, I got an email that I initially thought was spam. The
subject line read "20/20." I opened the email, and it said, "Hey Justin, we've
come across your story and love what you and Trish are doing to help other
couples. We'd love to talk to you about featuring you guys on *ABC News
20/20*." The messenger signed the email as the executive producer of ABC
News and left her phone number for me to call her. I wasn't sure it was true,
but I began to process how ABC News could have heard about our ministry.
*Maybe she's read our book, and it changed her life. Maybe someone on her staff
heard us speak, and it really impacted them. Maybe one of the churches we've
spoken at called ABC News and told her how much our talk impacted their
church.*

I called her, and after I introduced myself, I said, "Is this for real?"

She said, "Yes, this is very real. We love your story and would love to talk
to you about featuring you on *20/20*."

I said, "Well, how did you hear about us?"

She said, "Well, I Googled 'pastors that struggle with porn,' and your picture popped up."

That will keep you humble.

What if the thing that was the most painful, most shameful, most embarrassing part of your story could bring the most people freedom? What if God could use your eating disorder to help others who have eating disorders? What if God could use your divorce to help other couples avoid divorce? What if God could use your bankruptcy to help others avoid financial mistakes? What if God could use your porn addiction to help others find freedom? What if God could use your sexual abuse to help others find hope and healing from their abuse?

Jennie Allen wrote this in *Nothing to Prove*: "You know what happens when you are free? Other people are set free. When you put your dirt out first, everybody else gets to do the same. It's contagious. Other people are freed through our honesty and confession."[7]

> What if the thing that was the most painful, most shameful, most embarrassing part of your story could bring the most people freedom?

Somehow we think God wants us to hide the broken parts of us, or He can't use the broken parts of us, but it's actually the broken parts of us that have been transformed by God that demonstrate God's grace the most.

Guilt is not your identity.

Shame doesn't define you.

Brokenness isn't weakness.

Redemption is your story.

Transparency is your path to transformation.

God doesn't use perfect people; He uses authentic people. God recruits people from the pit, not the platform. Perfection isn't the goal of the Christian life—being real is.

Trisha Davis: While I know this book is dedicated to you, I wanted to say thank you for your support during this process. Thank you for believing in me and encouraging me to pour my heart into this book. While your name isn't on the cover, it's written on every page.

Micah, Elijah, Isaiah, and daughter-in-law Rylei: Thank you for loving me in this year's deep losses and celebrating the incredible victories with me. You gave me the courage to write this book. Thank you!

Janiyah: You are, without a doubt, my favorite daughter. Always remember your daddy loves you.

Jailyn: Thank you for adopting me as your dad. No matter what, I love you unconditionally.

Meredith Boaz: Thank you, sister, for loving me, listening to me, and reminding me that I am not alone. You are my favorite (and I think my only) sister.

Dan Balow and the Steve Laube Agency: Thank you for believing in me and the message of this book. I can be a control freak sometimes, so your patience in this process is much appreciated. I can't wait to see what's next!

Michael Covington and the David C Cook team: I knew from our first meeting on Zoom that you were the partner I wanted for this project. Thank you for stewarding this message and helping craft and shape it for God to use in the hearts of others.

Michael Chiarelli and the Paterson Center: You were not only a life-planning partner in one of the most challenging seasons of my life, you were also a life preserver, throwing me a line of hope and reassuring me that God had something for me on the other side of my pain. Thank you!

Brian Harvey: Thank you for being my counselor and friend. This book doesn't exist without your wisdom, tough love, and words of encouragement. God tangibly used you to help me find light in the tunnel and hope for the future.

Derwin Gray: Thank you, Derwin, for being my pastor, my brother and friend. Thank you for phone calls just to check in and text messages to offer encouragement. Thank you for writing the foreword to this book; your investment in my life means so much.

Aaron Brockett: Thank you for your continued friendship and support. You have been a listening ear, a trusted confidant, and a safe place to be real.

Josh Hussmann: Your selfless leadership, unwavering support, and commitment to being my friend even when I had nothing to give in return is a gift I will never forget. Thank you for being a multiplier of God's grace in my life.

Jeff Henderson: Jeff, you are not just the leader of The FOR Company; you are the embodiment of being FOR others. Thank you for sending flowers, for P. F. Chang's dinners, movie-theater popcorn, and countless other gifts that no one will ever see. Your encouragement was oxygen to me.

Chris and Cindy Johnson: Thank you for twenty years of friendship, for loving me unconditionally, and always being in my corner. I hope to be as good a friend as you've been to me.

Greg Lee: Thank you, Greg, for being a picture of humility and faithfulness to God, to the Church, to your family, and to me. I admire you and owe much of my ministry to you, as you repeatedly said, "I'm in it with you, Justin." You are a brother to me.

To my Hope City Church family: Words can't express how grateful I am for my six years as your pastor. I hope you can see how God used our time together to give birth to the message of this book. Your impact on my life is woven into every page of this book—much love.

chapter 1: who we pretend to be

1. Brennan Manning, *Abba's Child: The Cry of the Heart for Intimate Belonging* (Colorado Springs: NavPress, 2002), Kindle edition, 25.

2. John Ortberg, *The Me I Want to Be: Becoming God's Best Version of You* (Grand Rapids, MI: Zondervan, 2010), 28.

3. Reply to a letter from a high school editor, published in *High School Spectator* (Grand Rapids, MI), October 26, 1955. From *E. E. Cummings: A Miscellany*, rev. and ed. George J. Firmage (New York: October House, 1965).

chapter 2: do we really want authenticity?

1. Andrew Hutchinson, "Rising Social App BeReal Is Gaining Momentum, with Downloads Up 315 Percent This Year," *Social Media Today*, April 11, 2022, www.socialmediatoday.com/news/rising-social-app-bereal-is-gaining -momentum-with downloads-up-315-this-y/621929/.

2. Megan McCluskey, "BeReal Won't Save Us from Social Media—Yet," *Time*, August 4, 2022, https://time.com/6201636/bereal-popularity-challenges/.

3. *Merriam-Webster's Online Dictionary*, s.v. "authentic," www.merriam-webster .com/dictionary/authentic.

4. Claudia Hammond, "Do You Inherit the Ability to Roll Your Tongue?," BBC, January 30, 2018, www.bbc.com/future/article/20180130-do-you-inherit-the -ability-to-roll-your-tongue.

5. *Merriam-Webster's Online Dictionary*, s.v. "duplicity," www.merriam-webster .com/dictionary/duplicity.

6. United States Census Bureau, "Historical Living Arrangements of Children," November 22, 2021, www.census.gov/library/visualizations/time-series/demo /children-historical-time-series.html.

7. "Fast Facts: Preventing Child Sexual Abuse," Centers for Disease Control and Prevention, April 6, 2022, www.cdc.gov/violenceprevention/childsexualabuse /fastfact.html.

8. Lydia Saad, "Substance Abuse Hits Home for Close to Half of Americans," Gallup, October 14, 2019, https://news.gallup.com/poll/267416/substance -abuse-hits-home-close-half-americans.aspx.

9. Brené Brown, *Daring Greatly: How the Courage to Be Vulnerable Transforms the Way We Live, Love, Parent, and Lead* (New York: Penguin, 2012), 37.

10. *Merriam-Webster's Online Dictionary*, s.v. "humility," www.merriam-webster .com/dictionary/humility.

11. Rick Warren, *The Purpose-Driven Life: What on Earth Am I Here For?* (Grand Rapids, MI: Zondervan, 2002), 148.

chapter 3: come out of hiding

1. Steve Carter, *The Thing Beneath the Thing: What's Hidden Inside (and What God Helps Us Do about It)* (Nashville, TN: Thomas Nelson, 2021), 46.

chapter 4: realize brokenness is not weakness

1. Trent C. Butler, *Luke*, Holman New Testament Commentary, vol. 3, ed. Max Anders (Nashville, TN: Broadman & Holman, 2000), 109.

2. Leon Morris, *Luke: An Introduction and Commentary*, Tyndale New Testament Commentaries, vol. 3 (Downers Grove, IL: InterVarsity, 1988), 166.

3. John Ortberg, "Christianity Illustrated: Heart-Healing Forgiveness," sermon, Willow Creek Community Church, May 6, 1998.

4. Eric Mason, "Restored through Brokenness," YouTube, October 31, 2018, www.youtube.com/watch?v=NR4kx7JIRGs.

5. Crawford Loritts, "Experiencing God's Power," sermon, Dallas Theological Seminary, YouTube, May 9, 2012, www.youtube.com/watch?v=AD6uzyewXGg.

6. Martin H. Manser, *Dictionary of Bible Themes: The Accessible and Comprehensive Tool for Topical Studies*, Logos Bible Software (London, UK: Martin Manser, 2009).

chapter 5: let go of people-pleasing

1. Mike Bechtle, *The People Pleaser's Guide to Loving Others without Losing Yourself* (Grand Rapids, MI: Baker, 2021), Kindle edition, 33–34.

2. Derwin Gray, "Beneath the Surface: People Pleasing," sermon, Transformation Church, January 10, 2021, YouTube, www.youtube.com /watch?v=_fjbCXPgVRo.

3. *Merriam-Webster's Online Dictionary*, s.v. "insecurity," www.merriam-webster .com/dictionary/insecurity?src=search-dict-box.

4. Shawn Johnson, *Attacking Anxiety: From Panicked and Depressed to Alive and Free* (Nashville, TN: Thomas Nelson, 2022), Kindle edition, 171.

5. Deb Knobelman, "Research Confirms That No One Is Really Thinking about You," Ascent Publication, Medium, May 6, 2019, https://medium.com/the -ascent/research-confirms-that-no-one-is-really-thinking-about-you -f6e7b09c458.

6. Shawn Johnson and Andrew East, interviewed by Jeanine Amapola, "Professional Athletes Give Marriage and Life Advice," *Happy and Healthy*, podcast, https://podcasts.apple.com/us/podcast/professional-athletes-give -marriage-life-advice-with/id1515971195?i=1000551190223.

7. ProjectBEAR, "A sad book devoid of the Gospel. Read something else," review, November 11, 2015; Cyn Rogalski, "Was an OK book," review, March 1, 2015; Laura, "Don't bother with this book," review, January 26, 2013, *"Beyond Ordinary* Customer Reviews," Amazon, www.amazon.com/product-reviews /1414372272/ref=acr_dp_hist_1?ie=UTF8&filterByStar=one_star &reviewerType=all_reviews#reviews-filter-bar.

chapter 6: be brutally honest with God

1. Colin G. Kruse, *John: An Introduction and Commentary*, Tyndale New Testament Commentaries, vol. 4 (Downers Grove, IL: InterVarsity, 2003), 244.

2. *Psychology Today*, "Empathy," accessed March 27, 2023, www.psychologytoday.com/us/basics/empathy.

chapter 7: give away your shame

1. *Merriam-Webster's Online Dictionary*, s.v. "shame," www.merriam-webster .com/dictionary/shame.

2. Lewis Smedes, *Shame and Grace: Healing the Shame We Don't Deserve* (Grand Rapids, MI: Zondervan, 1993), 9.

3. Smedes, *Shame and Grace*, 6.

4. Smedes, *Shame and Grace*, 83.

5. Aaron Earls, "Most Teenagers Drop Out of Church When They Become Young Adults," Lifeway Research, January 15, 2019, https://research.lifeway.com/2019/01/15/most-teenagers-drop-out-of-church-as-young-adults/.

chapter 8: rediscover your identity

1. *Cambridge Dictionary*, s.v. "self-esteem," https://dictionary.cambridge.org/us/dictionary/english/self-esteem.

2. Kendra Cherry, "What Is Self-Esteem?," Verywell Mind, November 7, 2022, www.verywellmind.com/what-is-self-esteem-2795868.

3. Craig Groeschel, *Winning the War in Your Mind: Change Your Thinking, Change Your Life* (Grand Rapids, MI: Zondervan, 2021), Kindle edition, 12.

4. Adam Nourgney, David E. Sanger, Johanna Barr, "Hawaii Panics after Alert about Incoming Missile Is Sent in Error," January 13, 2018, www.nytimes.com/2018/01/13/us/hawaii-missile.html.

5. Chris Kolmar, "Twenty-Four Powerful Cosmetics Industry Statistics (2023)," Zippia, March 2, 2023, www.zippia.com/advice/cosmetics-industry-statistics/.

6. Statista Research Department, "Hair Care Product and Shampoo Market in the US," Statista, February 16, 2022, www.statista.com/topics/4552/hair-care-product-market-in-the-us/#topicHeader__wrapper'.

7. "2022: How Much Do Americans Spend on Their Health and Fitness in the Post-Covid Era?," ATH, December 16, 2022, www.athsport.co/blogs/news/how-much-do-americans-spend-on-their-health-and-fitness#:~:text=FIRST%20THINGS%20FIRST%2C%20AMERICANS%20LOVE%20TO%20LOSE%20WEIGHT&text=But%20it%20makes%20perfect%20sense,weight%20loss%20products%20each%20year!.

8. Daniel DeNoon, "Early Retirement, Early Death?," WebMD, October 20, 2005, www.webmd.com/healthy-aging/news/20051020/early-retirement-early-death.

9. Derrick Grant, "Why Do Retirees Die Soon after Retirement?," Elder Guru, accessed March 8, 2023, www.elderguru.com/why-do-retirees-die-soon-after-retirement/.

10. Shawn Johnson, *Attacking Anxiety: From Panicked and Depressed to Alive and Free* (Nashville, TN: Thomas Nelson, 2022), Kindle edition, 170–71.

11. This is a common translation of a quote from Johann Wolfgang von Goethe's novel *Wilhelm Meisters Lehrjahre*, vol. 4, bk. 8 (Frankfurt and Leipzig, 1801), 194.

12. Henri Nouwen, *Life of the Beloved* (New York: Crossroad, 1992), 21.

13. Jack Guy and Saskya Vandoorne, "Medieval Masterpiece Found in French Kitchen Sells for Over $26M," CNN, October 28, 2019, www.cnn.com/style /article/cimabue-masterpiece-discovered-scli-intl/index.html.

chapter 9: taking off our masks

1. Louis Keen, "A Timeline of Kyrie Irving's Antisemitism Controversy," Forward, December 12, 2022, https://forward.com/news/sports/523668 /kyrie-irving-antisemitism-controversy-timeline-suspension-video/.

2. Jon Blistein, "Kyrie Irving Boosts Antisemitic Movie Peddling 'Jewish Slave Ships,'" *Rolling Stone*, October 29, 2022, www.rollingstone.com/culture/culture -news/kyrie-irving-boosts-antisemitic-movie-peddling-jewish-slave-ships -theory-1234620125/.

3. *Merriam-Webster's Online Dictionary*, s.v. "sincere," www.merriam-webster .com/dictionary/sincere.

4. *Cambridge Dictionary*, s.v. "sincere," https://dictionary.cambridge.org/us /dictionary/english/sincere.

5. Dictionary.com, s.v. "sincere," www.dictionary.com/browse/sincere.

6. *Collins Dictionary*, s.v. "sincere," www.collinsdictionary.com/us/dictionary /english/sincere.

7. Steve Carter, *The Thing Beneath the Thing: What's Hidden Inside (and What God Helps Us Do about It)* (Nashville, TN: Thomas Nelson, 2021), 58.

8. Carter, *Thing Beneath the Thing*, 63.

9. Carter, *Thing Beneath the Thing*, 65.

10. Carter, *Thing Beneath the Thing*, 66.

11. Carter, *Thing Beneath the Thing*, 67.

12. Carter, *Thing Beneath the Thing*, 68–69.

13. Carter, *Thing Beneath the Thing*, 71.

14. Lauren Goode, "The iPhone's Face ID Will Soon Work with a Mask—If You Have an Apple Watch," *Wired*, February 2, 2021, www.wired.com/story /iphone-face-id-mask-ios-beta/.

15. Marvin Richardson Vincent, *Word Studies in the New Testament*, vol. 3 (New York: Charles Scribner's Sons, 1887), 307.

16. Brené Brown, *The Gifts of Imperfection: Let Go of Who You Think You're Supposed to Be and Embrace Who You Are* (Center City, MN: Hazelden, 2010), 49.

17. Trent C. Butler, *Luke*, Holman New Testament Commentary, vol. 3, ed. Max Anders (Nashville, TN: Broadman & Holman, 2000), 202.

18. Donald Miller, *Scary Close: Dropping the Act and Finding True Intimacy* (Nashville, TN: Thomas Nelson, 2015), Kindle edition, 65.

19. Miller, *Scary Close*, 65.

20. J. Ronald Blue, "James," in *The Bible Knowledge Commentary: An Exposition of the Scriptures*, ed. J. F. Walvoord and R. B. Zuck, vol. 2 (Wheaton, IL: Victor Books, 1985), 835.

21. Craig Groeschel, "We may impress people with our strengths but we connect with people through our weaknesses," @craiggroeschel, Twitter, September 21, 2014, https://twitter.com/craiggroeschel/status /513744135824502785?lang=en.

chapter 10: living a transformed life

1. Jennie Allen, *Nothing to Prove* (New York: Crown, 2017), Kindle edition, 202.

2. Larry Crabb, *Finding God* (Grand Rapids, MI: Zondervan, 1993), Kindle edition, 161.

3. C. S. Lewis, *The Problem of Pain* (San Francisco: HarperOne, 2009).

4. Brennan Manning, *Abba's Child: The Cry of the Heart for Intimate Belonging* (Colorado Springs: NavPress, 2002), Kindle edition, 159.

5. Michael S. Heiser and Vincent M. Setterholm, *Glossary of Morpho-Syntactic Database Terminology*, Logos Bible Software (Bellingham, WA: Lexham Press, 2013).

6. Manning, *Abba's Child*, 29.

7. Allen, *Nothing to Prove*, 202.

about the author

Justin Davis is an author, speaker, and pastor who has dedicated his life to helping people experience life change through the power of authenticity. He cofounded RefineUs Ministries, where he shares his personal story with honesty and transparency, inspiring others to find the courage to do the same.

Justin is the coauthor of the bestselling book *Beyond Ordinary: When a Good Marriage Just Isn't Good Enough*, which he wrote alongside his wife, Trisha.

He has spoken at numerous conferences, churches, and leadership events, inspiring audiences with a message of hope and transformation through the grace of Jesus.

Justin loves to spend time with his family. He enjoys playing basketball, indulging in the Great Wall of Chocolate at P. F. Chang's, and taking long walks on the beach with his wife and kids. Justin and Trisha live in Indianapolis, Indiana, and have five kids.